Economics
A Beginner's Guide

ONEWORLD BEGINNER'S GUIDES combine an original, inventive, and engaging approach with expert analysis on subjects ranging from art and history to religion and politics, and everything in-between. Innovative and affordable, books in the series are perfect for anyone curious about the way the world works and the big ideas of our time.

Economics
A Beginner's Guide

James Forder

ONEWORLD

A Oneworld Paperback Original

Published by Oneworld Publications 2016

ISBN: 978-1-78074-639-5
eISBN: 978-1-78074-640-1

Typeset by Jayvee, Trivandrum, India
Printed and bound in Great Britain by Clays Ltd, St Ives plc

Oneworld Publications
10 Bloomsbury Street
London, WC1B 3SR
England

Contents

Preface:
a beginner's guide
with a difference

There are lots of beginner's books on economics. Most of them are student textbooks. There are one or two 'general reader' versions of them – really, student textbooks with the mathematics taken out. These come in various shapes and sizes, but they are all very much introductions to the *study* of economics; they are the place to begin the process of *becoming an economist*.

That often seems to result in quite a bit of apologizing for the limitations of what is being presented. It is as if the student is told, 'Never mind that this argument is wholly unrealistic, one day you'll see how it can be developed to be more realistic.' Or a few lines, or even a coloured box, on 'the latest research' gives reassurance both that everything is OK with economics, and once the first book has been read, it will be great fun to learn more. Well, the young want to be enthused, and anyway, here's an obvious piece of economics: few lecturers will recommend a book that puts their students off their subject. So, if you want to make any money as a textbook author, you had better not do that.

That aspect of *advocating* economics is even more in evidence in what is sometimes called 'recreational economics'. These are presentations of economics which, with cleverly crafted and often ingenious arguments, show, or purport to show, that snippets of economic reasoning will answer all kinds of puzzles about the

world, including many that do not initially look like problems
of economics at all. Whether it is the murder rate in Alabama,
or the possibility that shy people being more promiscuous could
lead to the elimination of AIDS, the subject is presented as if,
whatever the question might be, the answer is sure to be found
in economics. Economics shows us 'the logic of life' or even 'the
hidden side of everything'!

It would be handy if it did. I suppose the idea that it might
was more attractive before 2007 than it has been since. But all
that confidence that we had reached an age of tranquility and the
end of boom and bust turned out to be rather badly misplaced.
There are now any number of economists' explanations of the
failure of economists to see what was going on, much less control
it. The argument about what went wrong will go on and on, but
it is too late to change the fact that everyone has learned how
unwise it is to believe everything economists say. It is just not
true that economists have all the answers, and there is no reason
to expect that to change.

There are other views of economics, of course. One seems
to regard the whole thing as the progeny of some kind of capitalist conspiracy. In these presentations it is as if economics is in
its nature about the advocacy of the free market, inequality, the
domination of government by big business, and possibly pollution – or some such list. Another view – still not a friendly one
from the point of view of those of us who have spent decades as
economists – sees it all as rather trivial, just a matter of common
sense: 'it's all about supply and demand,' they say, and retire,
content with a good day's work. If that is so, the best idea might
be to forget the economics and stick with the common sense.

For others, the essence of economics is absurd abstraction.
I can see more basis for that. Economists do sometimes write
down ideas far removed from reality, solve some mathematics
and declare the results to be true of the world. Sometimes that is
just a brief interlude of farce, but sometimes it is dangerous.

To suppose *all* economics is like that is either a mistake, or perhaps a prejudice. But we do need some way to tell the absurd from the useful, and it is not always obvious how we are supposed to do that. Simply to say that now and then an economist makes a bad assumption takes us nowhere, even though it must be true.

None of these views – the favourable or the unfavourable – offers a sound way of appreciating what economics is all about, what it can do, and what it cannot – or what it should not be asked to do. My view of it is that there are indeed tremendous insights available. But it is better to face squarely the point that they are usually insights, not discoveries. They are ways of looking at things which reveal something important. But they are not in themselves the solution to anything very much. Most of those insights are about the economy, economic behaviour, and economic problems. But lots of the best economics is not so much abstract as metaphorical. And those metaphors do sometimes provide insight beyond economics itself. Appreciation of the power of these tools is the key to seeing what economists are on about – or what they are on about when they are worth listening to – and what it is that can make economics an exciting subject.

Recognizing the metaphorical character of much economics is the first stage. The next, something which is often not taken seriously at all, is that of *interpreting* economic theory – or interpreting the metaphor, if you like. Only having done that are we in any position to *assess* it. And it is the assessing, in the light of the various possible interpretations, which is the key to appreciating it. And it is not, to be clear, either a matter of saying that this or that assumption is false; or of declaring that 'of course, people might not be rational' or 'there might be non-economic factors (whatever they are) to consider'. Of course, there are false assumptions and other factors. What we need is a sense of the limits of the metaphor in the argument; an appreciation of which aspects of a problem are being effectively captured by it, which are not, and which ones matter.

The good news about that is that anyone can have a go. In particular, about ninety-nine percent of the time, the only mathematics that is required is the ability to add up, subtract, multiply, and to compare two fractions to see which one is bigger (and, I suppose, to understand expressions like 'ninety-nine percent'). For the appreciation of the vast bulk of worthwhile or potentially worthwhile economic theory, what is required is a certain amount of logical thinking, an acquaintance with the realities of the ways of the world, a willingness to say 'rubbish' when that is appropriate, and, on the other hand, a willingness to see the insight in a metaphor.

And beyond that, there is a another stage, the least noticed of all. Economic analysis raises some big issues, and big challenges in social thought. Some of them are about policy matters – about what should be done. But some of them are much broader than that – they are more like matters of social philosophy; of how we conceive our society, as an economic society, and in some degree even more broadly than that. Most economists seem to have lost sight of the point that there might even be such issues, let alone that economics might offer some responses to them. Indeed, all too many economists are much more interested in their mathematics than any vision of economic society, and even for those who are not, the pre-eminence of mathematical presentations and the expectations they create blot out other things. But many of those other things should be part of economists' repertoire, because economic theory, if it is thought about in the way it should be, does address them. And again, the good news is that anyone can have a go.

So, in the pages that follow, I am aiming to present economists' ways of thinking, through a selection of particular arguments. The selection of topics is guided by what seem to be thought important topics in the subject, plus a couple of others

I think ought to be seen as responses to them. But I have also, of course, chosen issues that highlight ways of doing economics and so illustrate the frame of mind involved. Certainly there are plenty of important issues on which I make no comment at all, but there it is. The main lines are all well enough known to economists to be in the character of intellectual common property, so I have not littered the text with stories about where they originate. But I have included a brief note on the sources of some of the ideas, and the quotations in this introduction, at the end of the book.

What I am not trying to do, though, is to advocate economics and economic approaches beyond their true value. On the contrary, a proper understanding of the power of the ideas requires an appreciation of their limits. So, I am trying to suggest some ideas about interpreting and assessing the arguments; and about what the characteristics of the arguments are that expose their limitations; of how to tell good economics from bad economics – of when to say 'rubbish'. And, indeed, although all the arguments to follow are well known to economists, I would not go so far as to say they are all sensible. I shall point at one or two that I think are silly or dangerous. But it is also part of my story that, in the end, the decision as to what is good economics and what is bad involves significant elements of judgement and I cannot definitively answer that question. Everyone forms their own opinion about that.

I anticipate that many readers will suppose that the way to tell good economics from bad is to compare the conclusions of arguments with data. Actually, as will become apparent, the tools of thought – the recurring metaphors – of economic theory are not on the whole things to *test* at all. They are things to understand and interpret, things to contemplate and appreciate, and then to use or put aside as the case seems to demand. More than that, though, it is a sad fact that even when some proposition is advanced which seems to invite a test, it is a rare day when that process settles anything to general, professional satisfaction. There always seems to be another round of the argument, often angrier than the last, and no one changes their mind. That, of course, is not to say that, at each turn, the participants do not declare the matter settled. Certainly they do, but the conviction of individual authors is a quite different matter from the scientific settling of a question. It would take a book of an entirely different kind to argue that point fully, but since it is so hard to find really convincing 'tests' of pieces of theory, even when the character of the theory suggests that might be possible, I have not sought to present evidence of that kind at all.

So this is a beginner's guide to economics, but not to the study of economics – read a textbook for that – nor to the adoration of economics. It is in part – or I hope it is – more like a beginner's guide to the *appreciation* of economics, and by that I mean the *critical* appreciation of economics. Beyond that, though, I hope to offer some useful ideas about how the economist's modes of thought might contribute to our vision – how they might, within limits, affect the way we conceive modern human society.

A great deal can be understood by thinking like an economist, but not everything. Exactly where the boundary lies is not something I would presume to say, but I hope all readers will end up agreeing that, with economic tools, they can see the hidden side of *some* things; and, as I hope to convey, in contrast to so many other beginner's guides, that understanding comes from developing some insight into the hidden side of economics as well.

1

Economics: the short version

There are four ideas which are crucial to economics. One is the idea of 'rational action', or of the 'rational actor', which is always at the centre of discussion, but sometimes misunderstood. Then there is the issue of what economic 'models' are and what they are for. Understanding those is essential simply for seeing how economists go about their business. Then there are two more substantive ideas which are essentials – the idea of 'comparative advantage' and of the 'price mechanism' and what it does. Between them, these ideas provide quite a bit of insight but they are also in one way or another the foundation of much more economic analysis. Beyond that, they also illustrate both the kind of metaphor used, and insights about how economic analysis can be related to aspects of a wider vision of economic society.

Rational action and the definition of economics

Economics is, as has often been said, whatever economists do. That is not much help, though, to anyone who does not know what they do. We might expect economics to be the study of the economy, and that is how it started, even if the originators of that study would not have had quite the same idea of 'the economy' that we do. A lot of study of the economy goes on in government and think-tanks, and the people doing it are certainly economists. In university teaching and research there is much less of that than might be expected. The study of 'economics' has moved on from studying actual economies – or simply moved away from it, perhaps.

Another possibility would be to say that economics is the study of markets, or 'behaviour in market settings'. Actual markets are probably studied even less often than actual economies. If we say it is the study of 'abstract markets', then that again risks conveying nothing useful since it just raises the question of how we go about doing that.

As things stand, and if we think of what people do when they study economics, I would say that the best short definition is that economics is the study of rational behaviour and its consequences. That does not capture everything economists do – there are some issues where questions of rationality do not really arise. And there are economists who specifically set out to study non-rational, or incompletely rational behaviour. What they say about it, though, is always that they are addressing a limitation of conventional economics, and that is a clue about what it is that economists mainly do.

That obviously raises a question about what is meant by 'rational behaviour'. All it really means is behaviour that is properly and effectively directed at some clearly defined objective, within the limits of what those concerned know or could work out. Very often in economics, the objective will be put in terms of maximizing something – maximizing profit is a likely example. So, a producer might be said to choose their price with the objective of maximizing profit. Then the point of emphasizing that they are behaving 'rationally' is merely that the price is well chosen to achieve the goal being pursued.

Almost anything might be the quantity to be maximized – along with profit, or personal wealth or welfare, there could be exam performance and museum attendance. Or the goal could be to minimize something – casualties, pollutants, spelling mistakes.

HOMO ECONOMICUS

Economists are often mocked – or sometimes condemned – for the idea of 'homo economicus', which means something like a stylized, ruthlessly calculating, selfish creature which does exactly what is required to pursue its own interests. Some critics say that the idea supposes we are dealing with a person who has no kinds of feeling for other people, no sense of responsibility, or obligation. There are two answers to that. One would be that there is an *aspect* of people, or some situations in which people find themselves, where that sort of view is very realistic. The idea of 'homo economicus' is just a label to say that we are thinking about that aspect of a problem. The second response is to say that we can treat the ruthlessly calculating individual as having all manner of concerns for other people, or social obligation. Charity workers who are trying to maximize the amount of money they raise could be 'ruthlessly calculating' about how they do it. In an extreme case, health workers who expose themselves to the risk of deadly disease can be thought of as fitting the picture of 'homo economicus'. They are certainly not selfish, but they are doing everything they can to achieve a goal.

So, *narrow self interest* has nothing to do with it. It does not really matter whether we say the health workers are pursuing their 'self interest' and that self interest benefits others, or we say that they are maximizing something else. So long as we understand what we are talking about, the idea of 'homo economicus' serves perfectly well.

Some of those obviously do not initially look like problems in economics. But the idea is that the same kind of analysis can be used for them all. The student who wants to maximize exam performance has to balance studying time, the advantages of spending a long uninterrupted period working on a topic, with the problem of losing concentration; and the amount of time spent, all told, with the necessity of getting enough sleep and perhaps even doing the washing. The profit-maximizing producer has to balance the costs of different suppliers with the quality of their supplies or the reliability of their delivery, and perhaps the number of people employed actually doing the work, and the number of those required to supervise them. The cases all have the aspect of there being some goal to be pursued, various ways of pursuing it, and a problem to work out which is the best.

It can also be that the goal in question is stated as achieving a balance between things – like having enough beer for the weekend without its being too difficult to carry home. Or we might be stealing the most gold we can from the bank without taking so long about it that there is too much risk of the police showing up. In those sorts of cases we can always devise a mathematical formula linking the various goals so that we can think strictly of maximizing or minimizing the value of that formula. But the maths is not necessary to an appreciation of the character of the problem.

Similarly, almost anybody or anything might be doing the maximizing. It could be a company or a person; the person might be acting as a consumer, or a worker, or an employer. Or it could be an Oxford college, or a government, or a tennis club, or anyone or anything with the capacity to form objectives and take decisions about achieving them. Any of these, then, might be the 'economic agent' under discussion – that is not a spy who is careful with money, but simply whoever is making the decisions to be analysed.

A reaction to that is that people are not rational, even in this limited sense (nor are companies, countries, tennis clubs, and the like). People have whims and fancies, inconsistent desires, emotional reactions, weakness of the will. They also, we might add, reason badly, send regrettable emails when they are drunk, and just get it all wrong. Maybe that is true, but there are two responses. One is that in order to learn how much behaviour might be rational, we have to understand the outcomes of such behaviour. One of the fun aspects of economics is finding ways of looking at things which suggest that seemingly strange behaviour might in fact be a rational reaction to the circumstances agents are in.

I would place more weight on a different response. That is to say that the question of *whether* behaviour is rational is secondary to the fact that it is rational behaviour that is being studied. Perhaps some economists actually believe people are always strictly rational, although they are crazy if they do. More importantly, the irrationality of humans does not make the character of rational action uninteresting.

That definition also brings two other ideas quite easily into focus. One is the question of scarcity. An alternative definition of economics is that it is the study of reactions to scarcity. That has a great deal of merit, and the point is that to make the problem an economic problem, something must be in short supply. There must be something that needs to be rationed, or we are anxious to conserve, or that, one way or another, we wish we had more of it. Indeed, problems of scarcity do set the scene for many arguments in economics. But it is because resources are scarce that the problems of rational action are interesting ones. If they were not scarce we would not need to maximize what we can make out of them. These resources are then related to another recurring theme in discussions of the essentials of economics – that is, the role of incentives. Again it would be possible to think in terms of defining economics in these terms – it could be 'the study of incentives and their effects'. In that case, we think of the gold thieves as considering the benefits of taking more gold and the costs of getting caught and how these things determine how much gold they take. If we change the incentives – by making the penalties stiffer, for example – no doubt someone's behaviour will change. But again, most of the time, the incentives are interesting because they are amongst the characteristics of a problem that shape rational responses to it. So, again, it is the study of rational action and its consequences that is at the heart of the subject.

The idea of a model

One much-mocked aspect of economics arises from the use of 'models'. So, what is a model? It is a collection of assumptions. That's it. The mockery arises from the mistaken idea that models should be thought of as attempts at accurate descriptions of reality. It would be hard to get further from the truth. Models seek to capture an aspect of a problem, and put it under a bright light. A model is not a description of reality – it is not really a description of anything. Sensible models are designed to highlight some aspect of behaviour in an enlightening way, and good models succeed in doing so. We could think of them as being a bit like poems. No one ever asks 'is the poem true?' or 'are its assumptions accurate?' Rather, the poem invites the reader to see things in certain ways. Whether a poem is any good turns on what the reader feels is gained from looking at things that way. But it is insight, or understanding, or appreciation, that is at issue, not accuracy, or conformity with the details of the world, or testability.

So, here is a model. It is one that is often characterized as 'more advanced' in introductory textbooks, but there is no good reason for that. We assume that second-hand cars of a certain brand and type come in two qualities – good cars and bad cars. The 'good' ones are known by their owners to be reliable, whereas the 'bad' ones are known to be prone to breakdowns – they are all of the same brand and type so that is all there is to it. However, this 'proneness', we assume, is learned by experience – it is not discovered by inspection of the vehicle. There are owners of cars who would like to sell them – half of whom know they have good cars, and half know they have bad ones – and there are potential buyers of them, but they each wish to buy or sell only if they can do so at a price which is appropriate to the quality of the car. We assume that a seller of a good car would be willing to sell it for $6,000, and a seller of a bad car for $2,000. Buyers would, equally, be willing to pay $6,000 for a car they know to be a good one, or $2,000 for one they know to be a bad one. Or, we shall assume, if they know that there is a 50-50 chance as to what type it is, they are willing to pay $4,000. And, to make this properly a matter of analysing rational action, we assume that all concerned have highly developed reasoning powers about all aspects of the problem, including the market circumstances and each others' opportunities, objectives, and capabilities.

There is probably a temptation to stop there (or perhaps it came earlier) and start thinking about which of these assumptions is 'reasonable' or 'plausible'. It is better not to get involved in that at this stage. The one point that might be worth making is that all of those assumptions can safely be regarded as false. If there are some strange car markets where some of them are true, they are not important enough to be worth worrying about, and there are surely none where *all* those assumptions are true. So, the question of whether this model is 'realistic' is settled: it is not.

Never mind for now. At this point, the model has been stated, and we are moving on to consider what can be learned from operating it. So, first suppose – hypothetically – that *all* the potential sellers seek to sell their cars and the buyers know that is happening. Since there is then a 50-50 chance of any particular car being a good one, a buyer will be willing to pay $4,000.

The problem there is that the sellers of good cars are not willing to sell for that price. That means the buyers can be sure that *it will not be true* that all the potential sellers seek to sell their cars – here it is the logic of the model that tells us that the initial hypothetical supposition cannot be correct. Indeed, if the amount buyers are willing to pay is going to be less than $6,000, the only *actual* sellers will be sellers of bad cars. Since both buyers and sellers can work that out, they know all the cars for sale will be bad ones – there is no market for good cars – and consequently the buyers will be willing to pay only $2,000.

It may perhaps seem that somehow the buyers and sellers of bad cars can be left to make their transactions, and the buyers and sellers of good cars should be able to get together separately. The trouble is that this seems to suppose that someone could post an advertisement simply *saying* they have a good car for sale, priced at $6,000. Of course, a seller of a good car could post that advertisement, but then so could a seller of a bad car, and we are back where we started. If there is nothing that *confirms* some cars as being good ones, then there cannot be a market for them which is separate from that for bad cars.

The next question, then, is whether, if we take that argument at face value, it is an interesting one. Here are some reasons it might be. First, whilst the buyers and sellers of bad cars are perfectly happy – they all make the transactions they want to – *neither* the potential buyers nor potential sellers of good cars can make their desired transactions. There are people who know they have a good car and would like to sell it for $6,000, and people who would like to buy a good car for that price. But the two cannot be brought together to make a transaction.

There is therefore a clear market failure. What the free market is always said to do – one of the powerful bases of its advocacy – is exhaust the possibilities of mutually beneficial trade. When a buyer and a seller both want to trade at the same price, the free market usually lets that happen. There is an obvious sense in which it is a good thing when that happens. But on the assumptions of this model, it does not happen.

In this case, we can also say something – perhaps interesting – about the diagnosis of the market failure. One view is that the problem arises from the asymmetry of information between the buyers and sellers. If everyone knew which cars were which, there would be separate markets for the two kinds, and no problem. Actually, if no one knew which were which, then there would be just one market, and we might suppose all the cars could be bought and sold for $4,000. So the asymmetry of information, not just the lack of it, is a key aspect of the outcome. Consequently, there is an odd and paradoxical aspect of the situation, which is that the sellers of good cars are disadvantaged by their knowledge. If they really could convince the buyers that they had no idea what quality of car they had, then a buyer would pay $4,000. But while the situation is as described, anyone willing to sell for $4,000 reveals that they have a bad car. The problem is, in a sense, that the sellers of good cars know more than is good for them.

Another way of looking at it is that it is the presence of the bad cars in the market that makes it impossible to sell a good one (or, strictly, to sell it for an appropriate price). Consider the case where there were only good cars (and everybody knew it). There would be no problem about buying and selling them. It is true that anyone who wanted to buy a cheaper bad car would be out of luck, but that is not properly a market failure since there are no willing sellers – the market has not failed to bring willing buyers and willing sellers together.

If the effectiveness of the market system is in itself something of any interest, then those ideas must have at least the potential to be interesting. The obvious problem, though, is that the assumptions are so clearly false. So, we must consider how we should react to that fact.

First, there are such matters as the specific prices I assumed – $2,000 and $6,000. That is clearly of no importance. It matters that the price for a good car should be higher than that for a bad one, but that is realistic. Similarly, the assumption that half the cars are good and half are bad is there to allow a specific calculation – but the numbers are only illustrative. The assumption that there is a precisely agreed price for each kind of car similarly simplifies the exposition, without in itself being important. If the assumption were that different sellers of good cars are willing to sell them for prices between $5,000 and $7,000, and similarly different buyers were willing to pay different prices, we would have a much more complicated story to tell. But the central idea about the effect of the existence of the bad cars on the market for good ones would survive.

Then there is the assumption that there are only two kinds of car. Here, with the model in mind, it is quite easy to see what the effects of making a more realistic assumption might be. Suppose there were *three* quality levels. What difference would that make? Quite possibly none. The three groups of sellers would be willing to sell at three different prices, but – hypothetically again – if they were all selling for the price appropriate to average quality, that would be less than the value of the best cars. So, in fact, the sellers of those cars would not be willing to sell. Our clever buyers can work that out, so the price they would be willing to pay would reflect the average of the values of the bad and medium quality. But then the sellers of medium quality would not receive full value, and so they would not be willing to sell, and we are back to the case where only the worst cars are actually on the market. We could try four quality levels, but the same argument would be available. In this case, the assumption that there are just two kinds is no more than a device for explaining the argument. Whether it is true, or even 'approximately true', is nothing to do with the insight the argument suggests.

The assumption that the buyers (or potential buyers) know the proportions of the kinds of car that might be sold is similar.

What matters for the argument is that they have some sort of idea, and understand that there are enough bad cars for it to matter. If a buyer thinks there is only a one-in-a-million chance of getting a bad car, then we might think they would pay $6,000 – or perhaps that they would be able to find a seller willing to sell for a tiny bit less than that. If it is *true* that there is only a one-in-a-million chance, then we barely have a model where there are two types of car at all. But if there is a substantial chance of a car being a bad one, then all we really need for the model to work is that buyers know *that*. Again, the details of the numbers do not matter.

I also assumed that if the buyers believe there is a 50-50 chance of a good car or a bad one, they will pay specifically $4,000. That can be handled in much the same way. Taken literally, it means they do not mind a bit of a gamble. It would probably be more realistic to say they do mind, and would pay less than $4,000 – say $3,500. That variation is certainly harmless to the model. It actually makes the market even *less* favourable to the sellers of good cars – so the indication that they will be unwilling to sell is strengthened.

In all these cases, the original argument seems very robust. Some points force compromises on us – it might not be the case that *none* of the good cars are sold for a price near enough to the $6,000 value to be acceptable to the seller. But accommodating others actually makes the argument stronger. Through it all, a key point survives: when there is asymmetric information, the presence of the bad cars impairs the market for the good cars.

That leaves two more assumptions needing attention – and both lead to wider discussion about economic theorizing in general. They are the assumption that all those concerned have the reasoning powers to work out all the relevant aspects of the situation they are in; and the assumption that the sellers know the quality of the car and the buyers do not.

First, the reasoning capabilities. That kind of assumption is made all the time in economics. It can take slightly different guises in different contexts but, very often, it amounts to saying that for the purposes of considering a particular model, we assume that the economic agents, whose behaviour is analysed in the model, behave as if they understand that model. So here, we have assumed that the buyers and sellers *know* certain things – such as that there are an equal number of good cars and bad cars that might be sold. But we are also assuming that they can then *work out* what it would imply for the price of the cars if in fact they were all offered for sale. Having done that, the sellers of good cars will work out not to sell. But the buyers can also see that the sellers will work that out, and hence work out what price they, as buyers, should be willing to pay for any car that *is* for sale. And if we were considering the model with three types of car, or where buyers do not like gambles, or any other variation, there is more to work out, but we are assuming they can do it.

There is nothing to be said to justify that as the literal truth, but there are a couple of things which might be said to justify that as a modelling assumption. One is simply that a few people making mistakes does not damage the general shape of the conclusions. In this particular case, if the assumption is approximately true, that will be good enough.

Another point, though, is that we should be cautious about supposing that if agents 'understand' the environment or can 'work out' the answers that must mean they actually follow the reasoning process. If you throw someone's wallet at them, they will manage to catch it far more often than they will be able to explain the equations describing its path through the air. And the way a plant grows towards the sun is certainly not *calculated* as the optimum thing for it to do, but if a scientist does make that calculation, the plant will turn out to have got it about right. Depending on what question we are addressing, the modelling convention of 'assuming' the plant makes the appropriate calculation may be perfectly reasonable.

The important question, then, is whether people have a good enough idea of the situation they are in, or are otherwise led to act as if they do, for the model to be insightful. So, for example, simply learning from experience will guide many decisions. If people pay $6,000 for a car because the seller tells them it is a good one, they may well learn a lesson. If they and their friends tend to be disappointed, it is very reasonable to think they will learn to pay less. By that kind of process the whole market can develop towards the situation the model describes in terms of 'rational action'.

In practical terms, of course, that process could take a long time and with new people coming into the market all the time, it might never do so fully. That is true – and it is a trap into which economists fall too often to think that such points can be disregarded. The cases of strictly rational action, and learned behaviour in an ever-changing population are not the same thing. On the other hand, in this case, learning about the market is only a support for reasoning about it – both factors pull in the same direction. So we might very reasonably think that the general sense of the model, and the insight it promotes, survives the criticism of the assumption.

There is a more philosophical point there too. If we step away from immediate factual issues about how such markets work, and consider the picture painted by the model, we might feel it is *more* interesting because it traces market failure to the rationality of agents. Surely it would be no surprise if things went wrong because the people involved were clumsy, stupid, or rude. But it is none of these. Nor did the market fail because the lights went out at the crucial moment. In the case in question, if anything, agents' stupidity might mitigate the market failure. It is on the condition of strict rationality that the market most clearly and most completely fails. It is precisely the penetrating insight of our hypothetical agents which makes it impossible to sell a good car, even to people who want to buy one. Quite apart from what we might think about the plausibility of the assumptions as representations of the world, that is a point of interest about the relation of rational action to the market system. From thinking about this model, we can then say that not only does the free market not always bring together willing buyers and sellers but that rationality, far from being the characteristic by which we overcome problems, can in certain circumstances be one of the sources of them.

So that brings us to the assumption that the sellers know the quality of the car they are selling, but the buyers do not. Although that might well seem to be a reasonable assumption, at least as an approximation, it is also an assumption that is right at the heart of what makes the model special. It is, as I observed earlier, the *asymmetry* of information which is crucial. And as I have just said, rationality can make things go wrong 'in certain circumstances'. In this case, those circumstances are precisely the ones where the sellers know the quality of their car, but the buyers cannot confirm it. If that comes into question, then the model really does lose its applicability.

Here, there is a serious criticism to be made, but it turns on careful interpretation of what is being assumed. It is all very well saying that sellers know more about the car than the buyers, but what the logic of the model requires is that they have a clearer idea about its quality than the buyers can achieve by inspection. So, indeed, at first sight, a buyer might not appreciate a particular car has no engine, while the seller knows that perfectly well. But it is not hard to find out. Similarly, if one of the windows is stuck, or second gear does not work, those faults are discovered quite easily. On the other hand, it might be that the carburettor is about to fail, and the purchase will be a disappointment to a buyer – but that is very possibly something the seller does not know either, so there is no asymmetry of information.

So, paradoxically, perhaps, the assumption that initially seems to be nearest to the factual truth – that sellers know the quality of the car and buyers do not – is the one that really raises a problem. And it is not that there is no truth in the assumption, but just that – properly understood in the context of the role of the assumption in the model – it might not be a big enough issue for it to matter much.

That point, however, leads to another one, which is perhaps obvious, but certainly important. It is that, although I have put the model in terms of 'cars', that is just packaging. The sellers of anything might find themselves in this kind of position. The *logic* of the model is quite separate from the packaging, and of course the acceptability of that crucial assumption that the sellers know more than the buyers may depend on what we are discussing.

One important extension would be to recognize that it could perfectly well apply just as much to new goods as second-hand ones. That is perhaps concealed from view by the prevalence of 'brands'. The buyer can sometimes be confident about the durability of a product – even well beyond the manufacturer's warranty – because the brand carries a reputation for quality. But that suggests that the value of branding arises partly from the asymmetry of information that might otherwise exist. So one thought might be that the argument tells us nothing much about used cars, but something quite interesting about the value of a good brand name. We certainly would not have reached that point by dismissing the model for its 'unrealistic' assumptions.

As it turns out, though, and as I shall argue later, very similar arguments apply to a variety of cases where the issue is not really about selling anything at all. Sometimes, the metaphor of there being two types of car can guide thinking in quite different areas. That too makes this model an important one.

Comparative advantage

The essence of economic activity is often thought to be exchange, and the benefit of exchange to come from specialization. But it is very much worthwhile considering just how that might arise. Let us examine another model.

Think of an individual with the capability of producing either or both of two goods. And think not actually of the price but, more precisely, of the cost of production. For the purposes of the discussion we can think of the costs being merely labour time – it takes so many hours to make one good, so many to make the other.

So, individual A will have a labour cost of producing each of two goods, 1 and 2. Let us – keeping it simple – suppose those costs are both six hours. That individual can make either one unit of good 1 or one unit of good 2 in six hours (or two of either, or one of each in twelve, and so on). Now consider another individual whom we shall suppose can make one unit of good 1 in eight hours or one unit of good 2 in four, and can similarly make two units of good 1 in sixteen hours, and so on.

I imagine the next move will not surprise anyone: so long as these two can get together, it would be a good idea if person A spends time on making good 1 and person B concentrates on good 2, and they then exchange their products. This is simply an instance of specialization.

So, for example, suppose they each have 2,400 hours available. If they do not trade, it might be that A would produce (and consume) a hundred of good 1 and three hundred of good 2 while B produces two hundred of each. That gives total production of three hundred of good 1 and five hundred of good 2.

Starting from that position, we can consider the effect of some specialization. Suppose A reduces production of good 2 by ten, thereby freeing sixty hours, and uses those hours to make ten more of good 1. B, on the other hand, reduces production of good 1 by eight, thereby freeing sixty-four hours, and can increase production of good 2 by sixteen. We then have, in total, 302 of good 1, and 506 of good 2. As if by magic, the total production of both goods has increased. There is then an issue about how the extra output is shared between the two, but the key point is that there *is* extra output – there are many ways of sharing it so that both A and B are better off.

The next move is a more interesting one. Let us change the numbers to make person B's costs of production eighty and forty respectively. Now, instead of being rather obviously the better producer of good 2 and the less good producer of good 1, person B is spectacularly poor at both. But if A again reduces production of good 2 by ten and increases that of good 1 by the same number, B can still reduce production of good 1 by eight (saving 640 hours) and thereby produce sixteen more of good 2. In this second scenario, total production is lower with or without specialization, but as far as the possibility of *increasing* total output by specialization is concerned, nothing is changed. Consequently, the possibility of making both A and B better off than they would be without trade is still there.

The key to understanding this is to see that in terms of finding gains from trade, the absolute costs of producing the two goods are not the important thing. What matters is that the *ratio* of the costs of producing the two goods is different for A from what it is for B. In both the examples above, for A the cost of producing either good is the same; but for B, producing good 1 takes twice as long as producing good 2. It is for that reason, and regardless of whether the costs are six and six and eight and four or eighty and forty, or whatever else, that the gains from trade arise.

It is for this reason that the point goes by the name of *comparative* advantage. Person A is comparatively advantaged in the production of good 1, and B is comparatively advantaged in the production of good 2. It may be, as in the second version, that A is *absolutely* advantaged in the production of both goods, but that is nothing to do with the argument.

As I have presented it, this is obviously a bare-bones account. But so what? An apparent limitation is the treatment of costs of production in terms of labour hours. But that is an assumption which is only there to facilitate the explanation. Whatever it is that makes up the costs, and however they are measured, comparative advantages exist when the ratios of costs faced by two producers are different. Similarly, limiting the matter to two goods and two people, for example, does nothing to reduce the insight arising from the argument.

With those things in mind, it could very well be argued that this little model provides the most important insight in economics, since the existence of gains from trade is so fundamental. The idea is often applied to the case of international trade. It might be, for example, that a technologically advanced country can produce both agricultural and manufactured goods at a lower absolute cost than can a less advanced country. Nevertheless, it will very probably be the case that the less advanced country has a comparative advantage in the production of the agricultural products. In that case, both countries benefit when the advanced country specializes in producing the manufactured goods, and the less advanced one in producing agricultural goods. It is equally the case that an accountancy firm will benefit from exchanging services with a law firm. Two members of a household can 'trade' doing the washing-up for doing the vacuuming just because they differ in their attitudes to those activities. In all this, the key is that the 'gains from trade' are pervasive just because the only case in which they do not exist is where the two parties concerned happen to have exactly the same ratio of costs of the two activities. That is obviously not a very common occurrence.

And the bare-bones aspect of the presentation of the argument also highlights the point that the source of the cost differences is an irrelevance – it might be a matter of natural talent, or learned skills. It could just as well be that the weather in different places makes some things easier than others.

On the other hand, there are some important limitations. Some factors are not discussed. In particular the model says nothing about how the gains from specialization are shared. That will depend on what price is established for the exchange of the two goods, and the story is silent about that. My presentation also presumes that, for each person, the costs of producing a unit of each good remain the same however many units are produced. It might be that, say, for person A it becomes progressively more costly to produce good 1 as the amount produced increases. That makes no fundamental difference, but might limit the extent to which specialization can be carried with any benefit. Or, the opposite might be case – the costs of production might fall as quantity increases – so one can be produced in six hours, but two in eleven. That is an important possibility, but of course it magnifies the increase in output from specialization.

ONE DOUBT ABOUT COMPARATIVE ADVANTAGE

The idea of comparative advantage is a powerful one and surely has numerous important applications. But it is not the whole story of international trade and does not in itself settle many arguments about the best policy. Here is one concern – another is considered in chapter 6.

If we consider the case of a world economy where living standards generally rise over time, then we are led to the question of how this affects the prices of different goods. Following from the example in the text, consider the case where rising income brings little increase in the demand for agricultural products, but a large increase in the demand for manufactured ones. Then the relative price of manufactured products can be expected to rise. One way of thinking of that is that each manufactured product is worth a larger and larger quantity of agricultural products.

Then, at any point in time, and for any given relative price of the two kinds of good, comparative advantage points to the benefits of specialization. But viewed in the long term, the country producing the manufactured goods can expect to see its income rise faster than that of the other country.

It is also much less than a full representation of reality since I have ignored all issues of costs incurred in the process of exchanging the goods. As economists say to each other, it has been 'implicitly assumed transaction costs are zero'. Those costs are important, but it is also important that they do not make a fundamental difference to the argument. Economists mean that the gains from specialization must be great enough to cover the costs involved in making the transactions and still leave a benefit. That will be the case when the ratio of costs of the two parties is sufficiently different. In a common-sense way we can see that if Person A's costs of production were 500 for each good, and Person B's were 499 and 501 there would be theoretical gain, but it might not be enough to pay the haulage company. In that case, there are no gains because the transactions costs are too high.

Some of those costs are unavoidable, some are not. The case commonly made for international free trade is precisely that measures such as tariffs create costs of trade which reduce international specialization. But the same point applies at any level. If, for example, a plumber is filling in his or her tax form whilst the accountant is mending a pipe, we might think something has gone wrong. Perhaps they both prefer variety. That case would be covered by what I said previously about the costs of production increasing as quantity is increased – each has run out of patience with their own profession, so the costs of another hour are too high to make trade worthwhile. Another explanation is that in working, they would incur a tax liability. The plumber must pay the accountant a pre-tax sum for the accountant to earn a smaller post-tax sum, and vice versa. In that case, it might be that the amount of time the accountant would have to work to pay the plumber (with a slice for the tax office) is longer than it takes to mend the pipe. It is just as if, in trading an hour of services for an hour of services, they must also pay a fee to a third party. In some examples that third party is a haulage company, and in others it is the government, while in others it might be a deterioration of the product itself, as it is shaken up, or goes bad, or melts, or whatever it may be. In these cases, the gains from trade are limited. The metaphor, we might say, is the metaphor of the haulage company, but it applies in a whole variety of cases.

The price mechanism

Talk of exchange leads naturally to discussion of price. Indeed, so central is the price mechanism to economics that some people seem to think it is all there is to economics and that everything else in the subject is just a variation on that theme. There is a danger, though, in being too quick to see the common sense of the idea and thereby miss the most interesting aspects of it.

The simplest version of the idea would say that price is set in market so that supply equals demand – price is determined so that the two things become equal. That, as it turns out, is only part of the story. But it does raise some questions, including definitional ones.

A 'market' is traditionally defined as 'a group of buyers and sellers in sufficiently close contact so as to establish a price'. That will do nicely. Whether it is playground swaps of Topps cards, international financial transactions, or an onion bagel from the supermarket, the buyers and the sellers are in contact one way or another, and a price is agreed between them. In practice, that might mean the seller advertises a price and waits for buyers who will pay it; or it might mean they haggle; or there is an auction; or just occasionally, the buyers advertise a price and wait for sellers to come to them. But in the end there is a price for which the seller is willing to sell, and the buyer is willing to buy.

Normally, the 'price' is a price in terms of money. In the playground case, it is probably not – if the cards are actually being swapped, there is no money involved. There is a still a price in the sense that so many of one kind of card are exchanged for so many of another (that might be one-for-one, of course). The international financial case might be of either kind. There, it could be that things such as shares in a large company are being bought and sold for money, just as if they were onion bagels. It could be, though, that pounds are being sold for dollars, and that, perhaps, is more like a playground swap.

'Demand' is the willingness and ability to buy something, and 'supply' is the willingness and ability to sell it. It is important that in both cases it is willingness *and* ability. In the case of demand, that sometimes causes confusion since it does not correspond to ordinary English along the lines of 'We demand fair shares for the workers.' In economics, 'demand' is nothing to do with urgency of need, or insistence on receiving something – it is simply the willingness and ability to buy it. (For most purposes ability to buy means ability to pay.)

If we consider two possible prices, common sense surely says that there will be more demand at the lower price, but more supply at the higher one – so long as everything else remains unchanged. This allows us to draw the world-famous 'supply and demand diagram' of diagram 1. The downward-sloping 'demand curve' and upward-sloping 'supply curve' (each of which may or may not in fact be curved) illustrate the idea that more is demanded, and less is supplied at lower prices. Then it is obvious from the diagram that there can be no more than one point at which the curves actually cross. That point determines a unique price at which supply and demand are equal. The price being known, we can then also read off the horizontal axis the quantity traded.

The price 'p' in the diagram is 'the equilibrium price', or the 'the market price', or 'the free market price', (or the 'market equilibrium price'!). It is of course the price where there is a 'balance' between supply and demand, which is what student textbooks tend to say. One way of thinking about what that

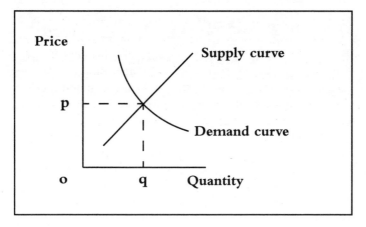

Diagram 1 Supply and demand

means is to note that there is no other price at which both buyers and sellers are happy to go on trading. There is, at price p, a 'balance' in the sense that if that price is the price prevailing in the market, and nothing relevant changes, then that will carry on being the prevailing price – the forces within this market itself are not such as to lead to any change. The quantity q is then the amount transacted at price p.

THE MECHANICS OF SETTING A PRICE

The question of how the price comes to be set is one that is sometimes thought important, although actually, the mechanics of that process need not hold much interest. Suppose we start at point p in diagram 1 and there is suddenly extra demand for a product. That would be represented as a shift of the whole demand curve to the right from D_1 to D_2. The *equilibrium* price is then higher at p_2. But it might take some time for sellers to react to what has happened. In that case they will continue to sell at price p_1.

THE MECHANICS OF SETTING A PRICE (*cont.*)

The result is that demand will be greater than supply – at price p_1, demand is now q_3, but supply is still only q_1. It must be, then, that some of the potential buyers are disappointed. Perhaps, for example, they get to the shop and find the stock is sold out.

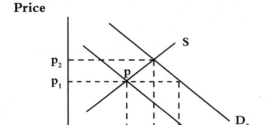

The adjustment of price

We could devise a model here to consider exactly how buyers and sellers will react to such an outcome. For example, buyers might accept their disappointment and go home, whilst sellers note the missed opportunity to charge higher prices, and when new stock arrives, charge more for it. Or it might be that the buyers, learning the situation, start offering more.

My view of it would be that unless we have a special interest in some aspect of the behaviour, there is no need to go to the trouble of *modelling* it. It is clear enough that since there are disappointed buyers, at least some of whom were willing to pay more than p_1, and there are sellers who are missing an opportunity, one way or another, the price will rise. (Had it been a fall in demand, rather than an increase, the same sort of considerations would apply, with movement in the opposite direction.)

THE MECHANICS OF SETTING A PRICE (*cont.*)

The key point about the equilibrium price is that it is the only one at which there are no disappointed buyers and no disappointed sellers. So, it is the only one at which there are no incentives to change the price, or make bids or offers to trade at different prices.

This does mean, however, that while we can say there is only one equilibrium price, we cannot confidently say that transactions never take place at any other price. People might well trade at prices which are not equilibrium prices. It is just that, if they do, there is going to be someone who ends up being disappointed, and that is going to set in motion events to change the price.

To say that the price is set so as to make supply and demand equal is, though, only half the story. To leave it at that would make the economy seem to be no more than a giant convention of stamp collectors, each trying to improve their own collection, but with the total number of stamps never varying. There is an all-important further part of the picture concerning how behaviour adapts in the light of prices.

All the while we suppose that it is desirable that consumers' desires be satisfied, the price system offers a very useful mechanism. One effect is that a high price will normally encourage economization in the use of a product. If we consider something like materials that might be used as an input in a productive process, then we can expect a higher price of a material to lead producers to use less of it. That might mean finding an alternative material; or perhaps being careful to pick up the scraps so that they can be reused; or it might mean researching and developing entirely new ways of making the final product; or even finding a substitute for the final product, so the use of that input in that activity ceases altogether. Equally, if the good in question is a consumption good, a higher price will lead some to consume less of it. To the extent that the high price itself reflects the scarcity of the good, or the high cost of producing it, these reactions are entirely desirable.

The question of the effect of price on supply is perhaps even more important. The vital point here is that prevailing prices (or prices which are expected to prevail) provide not just a reason for selling, but an inducement to producing. When the price of something turns out to be high – or high relative to the cost of producing it – then that high price is precisely what creates an incentive to produce more of it, and to find better and faster ways of producing more.

On both the demand and the supply side, then, the price mechanism creates incentives for individuals to behave in ways which are socially useful. Those incentives encourage both the economization and increased supply of scarce products. A spectacular example is the way in which the rise in the price of oil in the 1970s encouraged less consumption immediately, followed by research and development in fuel economy and alternative fuels, as well as the exploitation of hard-to-reach oil reserves, such as in the North Sea. By the same token, they encourage more consumption and less supply of relatively plentiful products since those are the ones with low prices.

The consequence of the price mechanism working in this way is that, broadly speaking, the productive capabilities are deployed in producing the goods consumers wish to have produced. A high price discourages purchase and consumption whilst encouraging production and sale: when consumers are willing to pay a high price, producers have the incentive to produce. Equally, when producers are unable to produce at a low price, consumers have an incentive to consume something else.

A further point concerns the immense complexity of the system that emerges guided by prices. We can consider something as simple as what it takes to get coffee in my mug in the morning. There are people growing, harvesting, and processing the coffee. There are people transporting, marketing, and selling it. Then there is a whole range of equipment used in each part of the process, all of which is made by someone else – probably in every case involving a similarly complex collaboration. And, we could say, there is the equipment used by those equipment makers, there is the construction of the buildings which are used, the roads which are travelled, the extraction of the resources used in fuel at various stages, and no doubt much more. All in all there must be people from all over the world involved in the process.

The difficulty in organizing such a thing without the price mechanism – by, for example, having governments issue the required instructions to the various individuals – would be prodigious. Yet the price mechanism accomplishes it pretty well. That is certainly not to say that nothing goes wrong. It is much less than perfect – the used-car example showed that, and there are plenty more cases to be considered in chapter 4. But whilst diminishing the importance of those things is a common fault of economists, allowing them to obscure the enormous power of the price mechanism is equally a mistake. The price mechanism brings coffee to our tables, and all that, *and* encourages the economization of scarce resources, *and* research and development of products or processes better meeting consumers' desires. Beside those things, the fact that it tends to make supply equal demand is not very much!

ELASTICITY OF SUPPLY AND DEMAND

The 'elasticity' of supply and demand is the measure of *how much* they change in response to a price change. The diagram (see p28) on the left hand side shows demand curves for two different products. D_1 is relatively elastic, meaning that a small change in price brings a large change in demand; D_2 is relatively inelastic, meaning the opposite. On the right-hand side, S_1 is a relatively elastic supply curve and S_2 a relatively inelastic one.

ELASTICITY OF SUPPLY AND DEMAND (*cont.*)

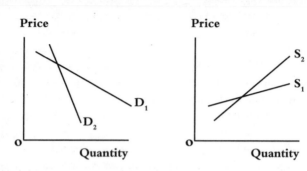

Elasticities of demand and supply

What sort of goods will be which? We would have to investigate the data to know. But it is natural to think of a high degree of elasticity of demand being associated with goods that have close substitutes, or are otherwise inessential or unimportant, or which are major items of expenditure, so that if their price changes it makes a large impact on the spending power of consumers. Whether goods do have close substitutes depends, of course, on what we mean by a 'good' – the demand for claret will surely be more elastic than the demand for wine, or alcohol, or commercially sold drinks of all kinds. Clearly the wider the definition of the good, the fewer the close substitutes, and so, presumably, the less elastic the demand. It is also likely that, over shorter time periods, there is less elasticity than over longer periods. For one thing, tastes may gradually change if something becomes expensive. But other adaptations can occur as well – if the ink for one kind of printer becomes expensive, those with that kind of printer may keep buying it in the short term but, when they replace their printer, switch to a different one just because of the price of the ink. Then the demand for the ink falls more over a longer period of time. Similarly, supply will be more elastic over longer periods of time because more adjustment can be made to the new prices.

Even that, though, is an observation about the science of the price mechanism. There are other observations about the social vision that might follow. One point is that there is an obvious and perhaps uncomfortable association between the price mechanism and the profit motive, and hence with greed. Uncomfortable as it may be, once we recognize the extent to which the guiding of production is the great achievement of the price mechanism, it is apparent that the profit motive is essential. In practical terms, it is the quest for profit – and the greedy quest for profit at that – which gives the price mechanism much of its power.

Another point, which was once a commonplace but has today been more or less forgotten by economists, is that one thing the price mechanism, in all its glory, does not do is give most workers a sense of their importance in the process, or a strong feeling of connection to the product they are making. That is a loss to society. Nor is the price system a trustworthy means to address moral issues. One question concerns inequality. It would be dangerous to suppose that the degree of inequality we observe is due to the price mechanism rather than to interference with it, or some deeper factor, but it is certainly a possibility and there can be no basis for presuming the price system in any form will give us the degree of equality that we might desire. Then there is the question of whether there are some goods (or services) that should not be sold at all. For example, organs of living humans are a favourite of moral philosophers, drugs of the political right, and school places of the left. The reasons are many and varied, but of course in every case the issue arises because the things in question *are* sold – and as far as the mechanics of the price mechanism and the profit motive are concerned, there are no moral distinctions.

Clearly, then, all is not well with the price mechanism. But before we move to other matters there are two other thoughts about it. One is that even though we might wish the price mechanism could sometimes be suspended, it can be very hard to achieve that outcome. One case arises when attempts by governments to control prices bring all sorts of unwelcome consequences. A much studied case is that of rent control. The idea of such control is surely to benefit renters at the expense of landlords. But how might it work? One obvious possibility might be that landlords withdraw their properties from the market. But what about these others – it might become a condition of renting a house that the tenants also rent the furniture. If furniture rentals are uncontrolled, they can be as high as it takes to restore the original rent. Or tenants rent the house but pay a further fee for using the garden. Or it might simply be that the property is not properly maintained. The tenants might like to move out – but to where? Other landlords are subject to the same restrictions. Perhaps the tenants end up doing the repairs themselves. But then they really are paying rent by other means. One response to all this is to say that, in the end, rent control works to the disadvantage of all concerned – including the tenants. But another is that if all these mechanisms work well enough, they might really make very little difference at all – they might just complicate the process and obscure the real prices being paid. In that case, *true* rent control is simply much harder to impose than it seems.

There are plenty of other variations, though. A bribe to a bureaucrat is plainly a form of payment. If it buys a licence to construct a building or import something, then there is not much point in saying that the regulation under which the licence is granted prevents the operation of the price system – even though that may be its precise objective. Nor is it really fundamentally different if the transaction is more in the character of an exchange of favours between old school-friends. And sometimes the transactions remain ordinary market transactions, displaced from one market to another – where good schools admit only those who live locally, real estate prices around them certainly seem to rise.

The decision that the school should not select on the basis of 'ability to pay' then comes to much less than it seems. So, like it or loathe it, the price mechanism is not necessarily something we can be without, even in cases when we feel it does more harm than good.

But the last thought is that we should also be careful about supposing that the character of the system provides us with riches by corrupting our souls. In many contexts the price system and the profit motive also reward enterprise and effort and they encourage self-reliance. More than that, they also induce cooperation. The people involved in any particular process, such as bringing bread to London, mostly do not know each other. Perhaps they would hate each other if they did. It does not matter – they end up working together. But when they do know each other – when they do meet – it is also worth recalling that a transaction based on price is not based on race or religion, or social class, gender, or sexual orientation. If we had heaven on earth, we would surely have no discrimination on those kinds of grounds. Failing that, the next best approximation might come from a pure profit motive. The pure profiteer measures everyone by what can be determined of their merit, skill, and determination.

Conclusion

So here is the short version: economists do it with models; the models are characterizations of problems faced by purposive, well-informed agents. They describe the objectives and the constraints on those agents and seek to identify the kind of behaviour that results from the efficient pursuit of the objectives. At the most basic level of analysis, we then find that it is almost always the case that two individuals (or firms, countries, or whatever) can benefit from trade. And if we consider how that trade is organized – with the price mechanism and the profit motive as its essential drivers – we see not only that those markets can produce very desirable results, but also that even if we think they do not, it can be a difficult matter altogether to stop their operation.

2
Three special markets

Having identified some key ideas in economics, the next thing – too often neglected – is to start to think about their limitations, or the limitations of the too-simplistic versions of them. These start to become apparent if we think about three special markets – the labour market, the market for financial assets, and markets for prestige or luxury goods. They are all of importance themselves. But of just as much interest are the different ways in which the price mechanism plays out in these cases – they are all cases where it may not be nearly as effective as often seems to be suggested. Even more notable, perhaps, is the importance of establishing straight away that economics is not merely about applying the same simple lines of thinking, no matter what the question.

The labour market

Perhaps more than any other, it is the labour market that economists – particularly when addressing non-economists – like to insist is just like any other. The expression 'it is all about supply and demand' is probably never more often used than in this context. Others object, sometimes to the apparent moral denigration of people as commodities – there is a sentimental resistance to accepting that the bare forces of supply and demand apply here. Sometimes the objection, although perhaps originating in the same feeling, is more to the idea that there is such a thing as 'the' labour market. Are there not many markets – at least one for each skill and location?

The economist's response is of course motivated by an appreciation of such things as jobs being offered to the best qualified and of the necessity for a seller of labour services to find a buyer. There is, after all, no 'supply of jobs' which is distinct from the demand for labour. And it is a fact – near enough a fact, anyway – that a lesser-skilled person, or a less hard-working one, or a less reliable one, cannot expect to be chosen ahead of better skilled, more hard-working, and more reliable ones, particularly if he or she expects to be paid more than them. Indeed, we deal in metaphor – why should the market for common muscle-power labour be different from that for steel girders; or that for management consulting from the market for tubs of lard? In many respects they are just the same.

So here is an important strand of thinking concerning the relationship between the wage workers are paid and the number who will be hired by a particular employer. We think of the labour being 'homogeneous' – that is, all the same – so that only the number of workers is at issue, not which ones. We assume that the employer has a certain amount of 'capital' – that is, a plant of a certain size, a known amount of machinery and equipment, and so on. And, finally, there is a 'market wage' – the amount the workers can earn elsewhere, which is known to both workers and employer. (Since the 1960s, it has always been a 'wage' rather than 'wage or salary' in economics.)

We can then address the question of how many workers are hired by considering the 'marginal product of labour' and its value to the firm. The marginal product of a worker is the increment to output brought by the addition of that worker to the labour force. The usual assumption is that successive workers add less and less. So, two workers, working with a fixed amount of equipment will produce less than double what one worker does.

If we add a third, the increase in output over what two could produce will be less than fifty percent, and the fourth will add still less.

There will clearly be cases where that does not happen – if some sort of teamwork is required, two workers may produce much more than double what one can produce. What is much easier to believe, though – actually, it is almost impossible not to believe it – is that, at some point, the marginal product of labour will decline. Two may produce more than double what one can, but two thousand will not produce more than a hundred times what twenty can; or, if they do, twenty thousand will not produce a thousand times as much. Or if it requires a team of fifty to be effective, five thousand will not achieve a hundred times what fifty can. If nothing else, they are limited by the fact that the fixed amount of equipment has to be shared with too many other workers.

So far we have considered the quantity produced. If we consider the price for which it can be sold, we would perhaps expect price to fall as more and more is offered for sale. Certainly, though, it will not rise. Consequently, if the additional output attributable to extra workers declines, the incremental revenue that the employer earns from selling the product of additional workers falls. If we assume that the firm pays the same wage to all workers, then there comes a point where the revenue associated with an additional worker is equal to that wage, and if another worker is hired, the extra revenue generated will be less than the wage.

At that point, hiring more workers will result in an increase in costs greater than the increase in revenue; but hiring fewer will result in a reduction of revenue greater than the reduction of costs. So, the number of workers the firm wants to hire is that number which makes the revenue generated by the last worker just equal to the wage. At a lower wage, of course, it would hire more – it would carry on hiring until the increment to the revenue attributable to the marginal worker had reached that lower level. At a higher wage, it would hire fewer people.

We can go one step further and consider the supply of labour – not to a particular firm, but in the economy as a whole. Here we shall assume that it is leisure, rather than work, which is valued. In that case, in selling labour, workers are giving up leisure. Then it is natural to suppose, and we shall assume, that the marginal value of leisure declines. That is to say that a person will be more willing to give up leisure, the more of it they have, or equivalently, they will become increasingly reluctant to give up leisure, the less of it they have. That is equivalent to saying that, from the worker's point of view, the marginal cost of supplying labour increases – the cost of the loss of leisure associated with the tenth hour of work is greater than that associated with the ninth. In that case, the hourly wage that will be required to induce a worker to supply a large amount of labour will be larger than the hourly wage required to induce a small amount. We have, therefore, an upward-sloping supply of labour curve to combine with the downward-sloping demand for labour curve – just like diagram 1.

On the basis of this we can say that the freely operating labour market will set the wage equal to the marginal product of workers, and that this will be equal to the marginal cost to the worker of giving up leisure. We can summarize that outcome by saying that consumers are willing to pay what they are willing to pay for the goods. This determines the demand curve for the firm's product. That, combined with the technology of production, determines their willingness to hire workers or their 'demand for labour'. This, combined with the willingness of workers to be hired, then sets a wage. So, it is the intensity of the consumers' desire for the goods, measured by their willingness to pay, which is at one end of the process that induces the workers to give up their leisure. A greater demand for the goods would raise their price, and hence the demand for labour, and hence the wage, and thereby produce more labour supply. There is, as it were, an exchange of payment for goods between consumers and workers, which brings us to the position where it is the desires of consumers that determine the value of work to the firms, and the balance of that with the value of leisure to workers which determines wages and the volume of employment.

That is called the 'marginal product theory of wages'. We could obviously argue in an exactly parallel way about the wages of a particular group, or the wages for a particular skill. And we could argue in a parallel way about the employment of 'capital' or 'land', as well.

FACTORS OF PRODUCTION

Textbooks often say there are three 'factors of production' – land (including all natural resources), capital, and labour. The origins of that classification lie in the fact that there were broadly speaking three classes of people. There were owners of land, owners of capital, and those who owned nothing of productive value, except that they had the ability to work. The point of the classification was to analyse questions about which policies or circumstances favoured the interests of which class.

Later on the same three 'factors' came to be used in the analysis of production so as, for example, to distinguish the speed with which the quantity of labour could be varied, from the time taken to acquire more machinery (capital). In this setting it is the physical characteristics of the factors, not the question of who owned them, that is central. In this case, sometimes 'entrepreneurship' was added as a fourth factor – it is the skill and capability of actually organizing the other factors of production to bring about production.

There is nothing sacrosanct about that classification of factors. Sometimes it is convenient to think of 'capital' and 'labour' because, perhaps, the point at issue is that some countries are capital-rich, and others have plenty of labour. Or it might be more useful to think of 'skilled labour' as distinct from 'unskilled labour'. Here, as everywhere, we are dealing in metaphor so we adapt the metaphor to fit the case.

Perhaps the most important of various directions in which this line of thinking points concerns unemployment. In the picture as painted – there is more to be said in chapter 6 – the wage is equal to the cost of supplying labour. There is no one who wishes to supply labour at that wage – or who would be willing to supply it at a lower wage – who is not employed. It is precisely analogous to the point that there is no one who wishes to buy a cup of coffee for the advertised price, and yet somehow cannot do so. Consequently, a worker who is not working is 'voluntarily unemployed', as it tends to be put in Britain and Europe, or not unemployed at all, as it is described in America. There is, in that picture of the free market, no *problem* of unemployment, any more than there is a problem if some people happen not to want to buy coffee. And, of course, as demand and supply change, the equilibrium wage will change, but so long as it does change, the unemployment – true unemployment, involuntary unemployment – would be expected to disappear.

That conclusion, though, depends on the wage changing to bring supply into equality with demand. Many things might stop it doing so – and in particular make it too high: minimum wages might, if they are high enough; resistance to wage reductions in declining industries; or unionization setting wages above the market-clearing level are all possibilities. Any of these might prevent the agreeing of mutually beneficial trades, and hence result in market failure. As with rent control, there might be ways round the fixing of the price; but to the extent it is genuinely fixed, mutually beneficial trades are prevented.

The relevance of state benefits or welfare payments to this picture is that they affect the supply of labour. Where benefits are higher than the wage that someone might earn, they are presumably unlikely to work. Where the benefits are nearly as high it is still the case that the person has to work for only a small increment to their income, and so again labour supply might not be forthcoming. Less often noticed is that there is nothing in that story which makes the fact that the benefits are paid by the state relevant to it. Those who have the option of being supported by their family are in the same position. The fact that some cultures seem to provide much more family support for the young unemployed ought to be seen, in terms of the bare economics, as creating the same sort of situation as generous state benefits. Some, perhaps, will condemn the family for doing as much damage as the state to the labour market; some may see a crucial moral distinction. But another way of looking at it would be to see the family support as the natural order of things, and the state benefits not so much as an interference in the market, but as providing the support that families no longer do.

VOLUNTARY AND INVOLUNTARY UNEMPLOYMENT

The argument in the text makes a clear distinction between 'voluntary' and 'involuntary' unemployment. A person who is unwilling to work at the wage on offer is 'voluntarily unemployed'. There are any number of complications that should be acknowledged. Some of these relate to the psychological realities of what sort of jobs different individuals will accept; some relate to the costs involved in starting a new job; others to exactly how the tax and benefit or social security system, and perhaps child-care arrangements, interact to affect the willingness to take low-paid work

One important issue concerns the point that, however much insight there might be in the marginal product theory, it can hardly be that people who have become unemployed find their way into new jobs *immediately*. In practical terms, there is almost always a delay. What is more, it is most desirable that there should be.

Suppose it were possible, whenever someone became involuntarily unemployed, to find them a job immediately, and suppose they always took it. Then there would certainly be no involuntary unemployment. On the other hand, many people would presumably be placed in jobs for which they were not suited. If the

> ## VOLUNTARY AND INVOLUNTARY
> ## UNEMPLOYMENT (*cont.*)
>
> alternative to that is for them to remain unemployed for a period
> of time and thereby find a suitable job, that could certainly be a
> better outcome for the individual, for the second employer, and
> perhaps even the first employer, who has a vacancy for a time, but
> then acquires a suitable worker.
>
> So it is very likely a good idea for those who become unem-
> ployed not to be encouraged or forced to take the first job avail-
> able. Whether they should then be called 'voluntarily' or 'involun-
> tarily' unemployed is not clear.

We can of course criticize this theory like any other. One clear
problem concerns the ease with which the outcomes described
might be achieved, particularly when some dramatic change is
required. Eventually, the system may achieve all such possibilities,
but the individual who loses a job can be severely disadvantaged.

Moving to deeper questions about the model, one particular point that has often been argued is that the firm's ability to
work out the marginal product of individual workers is highly
questionable. Even to say what the marginal product of a worker
is might be hard – what about a production line worker? If the
whole line is going to come to a standstill when any worker is
absent, then each of them has a marginal product equal to the
total product. But that cannot be right – if the firm was forced to
operate without a particular worker, it would reorganize things
to make it possible. Are we supposed to compare the output
under wholly different organizational schemes to determine the
marginal product of that worker? Those may be easy ones. What,
for example, is the increment to revenue consequent upon the
work of the cleaners? What about the people who decide which
pictures to hang on the wall in the head office? What is *their*
marginal product?

I think that an answer to that is that in some contexts, those are very real questions. If our focus were more on the minutiae of wage determination, or corporate decision making, or the organization of production – or on the science of management – then they would come to the fore. But if we give the approach a slightly easier ride, it says that workers are hired all the while those hiring them feel they get value for money from doing so, and the value that they feel they get declines as they hire more and more. If that is about right, the theory has something important going for it – the sense of the model, if not the literal form, survives that criticism of the assumptions.

So far, then, considering the marginal product theory of wages, it might well seem that, after all, the labour market is much like any other – it is all about supply and demand, with the 'demand for labour' set by its marginal product. Nevertheless, it is not. There are plenty of reasons for saying that, but in this chapter I shall consider two (and another of a quite different, and perhaps more surprising kind in chapter 6).

First there is that question of people's attitudes to employment and the sale of labour. Certainly it is not to be believed that if only the textbooks showed more sensitivity, somehow the labour market would be less brutal. No objection to hard landings can suspend the law of gravity. A different point, though, is that the sentiment of those engaged in these transactions affects how they behave. One point that seems to escape economists, but never anyone who deals with actual wage bargaining, is that feelings of fairness, as well as purer market forces, are particularly relevant in the labour market. The *feeling* that a wage is unfair reduces labour supply, both by leading workers to quit, and by reducing the care and effort of those who remain. These are actual feelings, which actually affect the acceptability of bargains, so the point is not a moral one about what the wage ought to be, but a factual one about the way in which feelings of fairness affect the willingness to work. Those feelings can, like the wage itself, be something arising from a wage bargain, but are then an additional determinant of the supply of labour.

A second consideration falls squarely within the normal bounds of economics; that is, not enough has been said about the supply of labour. It has been treated as limited by the workers' valuation of leisure, but of course their valuation of goods is crucial as well. They do not exactly – let us suppose – work for their wages, but for what their wages will buy. That means the relevant consideration is not the valuation of leisure, but its valuation in relation to the valuation of goods. That matters because the valuation of goods is – we might suppose – subject to the same diminution at the margin as it is assumed leisure is. The consequence is that, as we consider higher and higher possible wages, it is not the case that they will always call forth more labour. As the *hourly* wage rises, a fixed amount of work will provide the worker with more goods. That increase in the quantity of goods to be consumed lowers the worker's marginal valuation of further goods – or, as makes the point clearer, lowers the valuation of further goods relative to the marginal valuation of leisure. That factor pushes the worker in the direction of supplying *less* labour as the wage rises. At a high enough wage, a person will therefore earn so much so quickly, that they will want to work less than they would at a lower wage.

The force of that line of thinking can easily be appreciated like this. Imagine yourself being paid a ridiculously large amount of money per year. How many years would you work? And if you were paid ten, or a hundred times that amount, per year, would you work longer? What about if it were a thousand times as much? At some point, early retirement beckons, does it not?

Anyone who carried on working purely for the love of the *work* in those sorts of circumstances would be a very unusual person, but it might be said that there seem to be some people who cannot have enough wealth. That, I think, points to a different attitude to money. It is not, for those people, something that will buy goods, but more like a way of keeping score. They accumulate riches because it shows what wonderful people they are – they are proud rather than avaricious. Well, the existence of such people shows a limitation of the model. In so far as we work to earn in order to buy things, there will be some 'price of labour' at which increases will lead us to reduce labour supply. One way of representing that outcome is with the 'backward-bending labour supply curve' of diagram 2. In this case, unlike diagram 1, there can be more than one point at which supply equals demand.

That line of thinking can be applied in other areas – to the effect of taxes, for example. An increase in taxes, by reducing the reward for an hour's work, pushes towards less labour supply. But by making the worker poorer, it raises the value of income at the margin and pushes towards greater labour supply. This theory cannot say which effect will be more powerful for

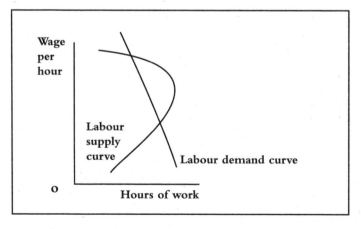

Diagram 2 Backward-bending labour supply

particular workers. It is perhaps plausible that poorer people will be induced to work more and richer ones less, although we cannot be sure. Well-off people do sometimes say they have to keep working so hard in order to have enough money to pay their taxes. Some of them are being sarcastic, but what they are saying is that, if their taxes were lower, they would work less (and if they were higher, I suppose, that they would work more). There is nothing in economic theory to say they would not, so one option would be to take them at their word – and set tax rates accordingly!

Markets for financial assets

Financial assets are one of those things with no very clear definition. But for most purposes we can think of them coming in three kinds: insurance, debt, and equity. Insurance has the characteristic that it pays out if, and only if, certain circumstances arise. Debt is supposed to pay out in all circumstances according to a pre-arranged schedule of interest payments and repayment of the principal. Equity holders are the owners of a business – so if there are 10,000 shares, the owner of each has 1/10,000 ownership of the business and is therefore entitled to that share of its dividend (or of the value of the firm if it is wound up). There are plenty of financial assets which do not fit neatly into just one of these categories, but the essentials of most are that they offer some combination of certain payment, payment if certain conditions arise, and a specified share of whatever earnings there are. And some, of course, mix elements of non-financial assets as well – like equity shares in an enterprise which entitle their holders to an allocation of free tickets to its events.

In terms of the behaviour of financial markets, most of the issues arise from considering transactions involving financial assets after they have initially been sold, and are then being sold or exchanged again. Only some financial assets are traded in that way. Simple insurance contracts, for example, are normally not: they are bought by someone who wants insurance and they either pay out or do not and at some point they expire. The simplest loans are an arrangement between two people, and that is all there is to it. Plenty of equity is also more or less non-tradable. For example, a consulting company which is primarily a vehicle for the delivery of its owner's consultancy services cannot really be sold – at least not if it means the erstwhile owner will stop doing the work. (Although if anyone wants to make a bid for mine, I am open to offers.)

That still leaves plenty of financial markets where there is a great deal of trading after the initial sale, and the first step in thinking about their operation is appreciating certain fundamental aspects of how they work. Consider 'bond markets' in which debt is bought and sold. What that means is that the initial borrower sells a 'bond', which is a commitment to making a future stream of payments to the buyer. The simplest bond would be one that pays a regular fixed amount – say $5 per year – forever. The buyer pays an upfront amount for that – say $100. In that case there is the exact equivalent of an interest-only, perpetual loan at an interest rate of five percent. However, having been sold to an initial purchaser, the bond can then be sold to someone else. When that happens, the price for which it is sold is something to be agreed between the parties, but not the borrower. So, they might agree a price of $90, but the buyer then still receives the $5 per year from the original borrower. That is the entitlement granted by the bond. The original purchaser of the bond has then made capital loss of $10 and the second purchaser of it is receiving an interest rate of about 5.5%, rather than the original 5% (that is 5/90, rather than 5/100). From the point of view of the borrower, though, the interest they are paying is still $5. An important point to appreciate is that the price of the bond going down (from $100 to $90 in the example) is the same thing as the interest rate going up – it is not even right to say that one of these causes the other: they are actually the same thing.

Perpetual bonds of that kind make the sums easier, but are in fact rather rare, simply because most borrowers are not expected to be in existence forever, although governments have sometimes borrowed on that basis. More common are variations where there is a redemption date at which time the loan is repaid and the regular payments cease, but there are any number of more complicated possibilities. A key point, though, is that there is always the aspect of the price of the bond and the interest rate moving in opposite directions so that we can think equally of 'the interest rate falling' or 'the price of bonds rising'.

If we ask a question as to why that would happen, then thinking of the bonds of a particular borrower – a large company, perhaps – the price of their bonds most likely falls because interest rates in general have risen, or because some doubt has developed as to whether they will repay the bond (or otherwise meet its terms). Should the company, for example, go bankrupt, the bonds may not be repaid (or be only partly repaid). So, changing sentiment about the prospects of the borrower will influence the price of the bonds they have already sold, making for the possibility of capital gains and losses for the lenders.

Something similar is true of equity. The shares in a firm that seems likely to become bankrupt will be nearly worthless. A sudden turnaround in its fortunes will see them rise, possibly very sharply. In the case of equity there is no regular interest payment, but rather a variable dividend payment. So, changing ideas about future dividend payments will similarly affect the market price of the asset.

These sorts of considerations – the financial stability of bond issuers, the viability of a business, and its stream of future dividend payments – might be regarded as the fundamental determinants of the prices of bonds and equity. The greater the stream of payments, the higher the price; the greater the likelihood of default or bankruptcy, the lower it will be.

In understanding the behaviour of financial markets, those fundamentals are only the beginning. A characteristic of the market for financial assets is that typically there is no impediment to very fast price changes – it is not even as if someone has to go round putting different price tags on the shelves. That means that news about any of the relevant fundamentals can bring price changes which are for practical purposes instantaneous. It also means, of course, that those who can anticipate the news might be expected to be able to make large profits. If, on Thursday, I can accurately anticipate that, on Friday, a larger than expected dividend will be announced by a particular firm, buying shares in that firm on Thursday would seem to be a good idea. When the news gets out, their price will rise, and I can sell them again, pocketing the difference in the price on Thursday and Friday (less transactions costs).

There is something in that, but things are not so simple since if the outcome has already been anticipated by other people on Wednesday, their buying will have raised the price. Indeed, in the theoretical extreme, it will raise the price all the way to the level justified by whatever news they anticipate. If it were any lower than that, there would still be a profit to be made by buying. So, if Friday is going to see an announcement by a firm of a larger than expected dividend, those who wait until after the announcement to buy the shares will find that their price is set so that the large dividend offers no more than a normal return. But those who buy on Thursday will find the same thing if the announcement was anticipated on Wednesday. The people who make the big money are those who buy before the anticipation in question is wide-spread. They buy at a price which makes the *previously* anticipated dividend a normal return. Anticipation is everything.

That point naturally makes financial market participants anxious to be in a position to form such anticipations – and to make them fast, and accurately. One very prominent strand of thinking suggests that they are highly effective at doing so. This, interestingly, has the paradoxical result that changes in market prices become impossible to predict.

This idea goes by the name of 'the efficient markets hypothesis'. The hypothesis is that market prices of financial assets always accurately reflect all available information that is relevant to the valuation of that asset. One way of looking at it is to say that if there is a piece of information which is relevant to the price of an asset, but has not been considered, then someone can use that information to profit. To take an absurdly simple case, suppose the market failed to react to the fact that a gold-mining company had struck a rich seam of gold. Anyone who did notice that would work out that the profits of the company would be higher than the market was expecting, and buy shares in it. No doubt in due course the share price would rise, but if not, then still the profits and hence the dividends would rise. Either way, the fast purchaser does well.

That really is an absurdly simple example – of course, the markets notice when someone strikes gold. But any other news has the same sort of effect. If a new managing director is appointed, then every detail of that person's capabilities in relation to the needs of the company are relevant. If anything is neglected, someone can profit by discovering it. In principle, even the question of anticipating who will be appointed managing director could be of interest – if it is going to make a difference to the profits, then in due course it will make a difference to the share price. If it is going to do that, then there is the opportunity to trade in anticipation of that change in the share price. So, since there is a permanent profit-based incentive to discover *all* the relevant facts, we might well conclude that they are all discovered and hence that the market price incorporates all the available information.

Prices of assets do still change, of course. But that happens only when there is 'news' in the sense of something happening that was unpredicted by the best predictions – and those sorts of things are random. Hence the paradox: the theory does nothing to predict market outcomes, but rather specifically asserts that they are unpredictable.

Another implication – not *quite* an implication, really – is that the behaviour of the financial markets offers the best available information about the quality of aspects of economic policy. When a policy announcement, for example, is greeted by a rise in the stock market, it is hard to escape the conclusion – if we adopt the efficient markets hypothesis – that the financial markets believe the announced policy will be good for business, and that it is therefore good policy. Similarly, if government bond prices fall, it means the markets have decided that the government should be paying a higher interest rate – that does not sound like good news. So it is easy to form the impression that the financial markets somehow know so much that their responses offer wise judgment on government actions.

How much confidence we should have in the efficient markets hypothesis is of course another matter. Some might be inclined to dismiss it as absurd, but before doing that we should be clear that there can hardly be *nothing* in it. The extreme case would be where no one was investigating the fundamental determinants of prices. But that would be a situation in which anyone doing a small amount of such research could make money doing so. Once those people are doing some research, very possibly the best way of reacting is for others also to do that kind of research. That idea seems to put us on the road to accepting the hypothesis.

On the other hand, there is plenty of scope for doubting the power of the argument. For one thing, whereas it is easy to accept the idea that accurately using all the available information is the best that anyone can do in the long run, the case that this is the best anyone can do in the short run is not so clear. Sure enough, if everyone involved in the market is assessing the fundamentals, then there is nothing to be gained by doing anything else. But what if there are some participants who are not doing that – perhaps they prefer to be guided by the patterns in the clouds. It may be that, in the long run, those individuals will be driven out of the market by their losses; but that fact is balanced by the well-known proposition that there is one born every minute. So, at any point in time, there might be such people in the market.

Furthermore, their views may be irrationally formed, but that does not mean it is impossible to profit by rationally anticipating those *inaccurate* anticipations. If, one Wednesday, I am able to determine that on Thursday market participants generally will form an anticipation that there will be good news about a certain company on Friday, then I can anticipate the price will rise on Thursday, and I can buy on Wednesday, planning to sell again on Thursday, after the price has risen. If I am correct, I make a profit no matter either what I believe about the news on Friday, or what the truth turns out to be. There, anticipating the anticipations does the trick in the same way as anticipating the fundamentals.

This point introduces a substantial difficulty in understanding the behaviour of financial markets. If there are a large number of agents speculating on the basis of their views about others' speculative behaviour, then their decisions can be very far removed from any appreciation of the fundamentals. But of course there is usually no way of determining in any particular case exactly what the thinking process of the participants was and, consequently, no way of determining to what extent their behaviour was based on an assessment of fundamentals rather than of the likely views of others.

Then there is the point that many of the people actually making decisions about financial market transactions are not rewarded in close relation to the results of their decisions. They are, for example, working for fund managers, and have substantial incentives not to deviate too far from the norm of what other fund managers are doing. Those whose funds they manage no doubt have some regard to the success of their decisions, but they are not in a strong position to assess the quality of decisions made except by reference to how they compare with those of other fund managers. So, from the managers' point of view, it may be better more or less to go with the herd than to base decisions on deeper analysis which might – in the short run – turn out badly.

In that case, there is a further interesting reflection on the operation of the system as a whole. The efficient markets hypothesis leads us to expect price changes to be random and unpredictable, but if no one is doing anything more than trying to look over everyone else's shoulder to see what decisions they are making, the overall results of that will be pretty well random as well. And since the efficient markets hypothesis suggests that no one can do much better than the market as a whole, it means that the competence in copying everyone else could be hard to distinguish from the highest financial expertise. So, perhaps, fund managers have every reason to be grateful to economists for the efficient markets hypothesis, just as economists find it very useful themselves when asked for market forecasts across the dinner table.

Whatever view we take of the efficient markets hypothesis, it probably does little to make the financial markets seem less mysterious, and probably not much to diminish the common impression that they are more or less just a racket carried on for the benefit of the participants and with no wider purpose. But if those elements are there as well, it is not to be forgotten that these markets have important functions. In the case of insurance, that must be clear. If it were impossible to insure a house against fire, we would all be worse off in having to live with that risk. Without life insurance markets, many people would again be exposed to large and unwelcome risks. Debt and equity are to some extent alternative ways of financing business investment. Without them, many businesses would never have started or not have grown. Debt is also a principal means by which many people buy a home or finance their education. Without these financial possibilities, we would be much worse off.

That though, is only thinking about the borrowers. A point sometimes forgotten is that one wonderful characteristic of the world is the possibility of lending by 'buying' financial assets in order to transfer current spending power into the future. One very important mechanism for doing that is the pension fund. Individuals make contributions while working; the fund uses those contributions to buy financial assets; those assets provide the returns to pay the pensions. Without some form of financial market, these things could not be done.

Prestige goods

In discussing the operation of the price system, nothing much has been said about the character of consumer preferences. They are treated as data, about which no questions are asked, but as being subject to satisfaction – in greater or lesser degree – by the production of the appropriate goods and services. This view supposes that consumers have given preferences and budget, and observe market-determined prices before making an optimizing choice of consumption. That way of looking at the question clearly has plenty going for it, and certainly puts the price system in its best light. It works very smoothly when applied to very simple problems such as how to spend a certain amount of money on a night out – food, drinks, perhaps the theatre … or more drinks. And we can make that sort of picture more complete by thinking of the labour/leisure decision by which an individual's income can be determined. Then, we have a picture, based on the idea that, given their preferences, consumers choose, from amongst affordable options, the combination of labour, leisure, spending on various sorts of goods, and saving that they prefer.

There are, though, various ways in which that analysis is incomplete. Some of them could be grouped as raising issues about whether consumers truly know their own interests. One such case arises over addiction. It is possible – arguing like an economist – to devise a theory of 'rational addiction'. The idea would be that the pleasure of the initial consumption is so great as to outweigh the bad news that follows. Most people, I suppose, will say that the less that is said about that sort of theory, the better. But it is not only addiction that poses a problem for standard economic theory – there are such things as wishful thinking, weakness of the will, and reactions like the 'sour grapes' feeling whereby people stop wanting something when it is apparent they cannot have it. Economists sometimes deny these things exist, sometimes theorize about them, but for the most part I think they should be regarded simply as being outside economics. They are aspects of psychological reality which are not under discussion – they are not traits exhibited by *homo economicus*.

But other limitations of the usual theory are closer to home. One of them concerns prestige goods – sometimes called goods of 'conspicuous consumption'. We can start with the case of goods which cannot be reproduced. For example, they are first editions of books, antiques, paintings by dead people. There is another category where it is not exactly true that reproduction is impossible but where the supply is fundamentally limited by characteristics of the good. These would be things like apartments with views over Central Park.

These are irreproducible goods – they exhibit 'perfectly inelastic supply', meaning that a price increase brings no change in supply. Their existence, though, does not suspend the price mechanism – it probably just means that the goods in question go to the highest bidder. Nor is it the case that there is any ideal solution to this kind of problem – it is not as if the fact that there is only room for one house at the top of the hill is the fault of the price system and could be overcome by some other arrangement. It is just the way things are. But those things should not distract us from another point. The great strength of the price mechanism is not that it is an effective way of making sure that rich people get the goodies – that is a consequence of it, not its appeal. Rather, as I was arguing on pages 25 to 27, much of the appeal lies in the fact that it directs entrepreneurial activity and productive effort towards doing the things that consumers want done. The existence of goods of perfectly inelastic supply disables that powerfully appealing mechanism. It also means that remarks like 'whoever can pay for it should have an ice cream' and 'whoever can pay for it should have a ticket for the men's finals at Wimbledon' are remarks of a quite different moral tone. They both recognize the effect of the price system in guiding the allocation of a given set of goods, but they do not equally recognize the value of the system in guiding the process of production towards the things that the consumers wish to consume. (And indeed, in these sorts of cases, including Wimbledon, the price system is often supplemented with other systems, such as a lottery.)

The distinction between allocating existing goods and producing the goods people want comes to the fore even more clearly as a form of conspicuous consumption where what a person desires is the biggest, or the fastest, or generally the mostest of something (or the biggest amongst their circle of friends, or whatever it may be). In these cases, only one person can be the owner of such a thing, but it is not exactly true that supply is completely inelastic, since bigger and faster versions can always be made. The problem here, obviously, is that whilst the desire for the big and the fast can be satisfied, if what is wanted is specifically the biggest and the fastest, the pouring of resources into the activity is futile. Only one person can have what they all want, and the price mechanism leads society not to an optimal allocation of resources, but to their waste.

It may be that those sorts of things are details. For most people, considering most goods, most of the time, the things that people want are things that can be reproduced. But a second concern arises from the implicit assumption that consumers' desires are 'given' – that they exist, as it were, before the consumer engages in economic activity, so that what the economic system does is react to them and, where it can, satisfy them. The non-reproducibility of Picassos does not challenge that, and we can probably live with the idea that some people have a desire for the biggest or the fastest of things, irrespective of what size or speed that entails. But along the same sort of lines there is another case. They are goods which, although they *could* be reproduced on an effectively unlimited scale, are valued by consumers for their scarcity, and for that reason are kept scarce by their producers. Branded fashion goods are a likely example, but there are plenty of others.

When we observe, as we often do, that the producers are not only keeping the goods scarce, but also advertising them, we start to see the producers in something of the role of creating the desires as well as the means of their satisfaction. The difficulty economic theory has with these goods is that they blur the distinction between desires and possibilities. The ordinary theory of consumer demand – briefly summarized in the first paragraph of this section – makes people's desires and preferences independent of what they can afford. But if the desire for a good depends on its prestige value, it might even be that it becomes more desirable as it becomes more expensive. Then we are in a different world. We are then not dealing with a consumer with *given* preferences confronting market prices and making appropriate choices. Rather, the prices are affecting the preferences themselves. And as a further point, we should note that in this case, the 'brand' is very valuable to its owner, but its value need have no connection at all to the kind of asymmetry of information under discussion on page 15.

These too might be thought to be exceptional cases, and perhaps they are. But it is worth a moment's reflection. I wonder how many people really buy a tie pin, or running shoes, or a carpet, or even just a shirt, with nothing but functionality and value for money in mind and not at all for show? Certainly, the 'bargain' which has the appearance of being a prestige good but which is actually cheaper, is often welcome. But where there are no bargains, how often does the impression that a purchase makes on our friends matter; and how often do we think that the cheapest functional version of the good will not impress them at all?

In any case, in all these areas – the labour market, asset markets, and prestige good markets – we can see economic forces, sometimes combined with forces not normally called 'economic', play out in slightly unexpected ways. It is true – it *is* all about supply and demand, but merely knowing that takes us practically nowhere. The ordinary price mechanism is a wonderful and powerful thing, but treating it too uncritically, failing to explore the ramifications and odd cases is something that can lead people astray. As with everything else in economics, we need to keep a critical eye, even on the most powerful pieces of theory.

3
Monopoly and competition

The idea of 'monopoly' conjures up an image of a large, powerful, and very probably exploitative firm. Perhaps the idea of 'competition' conjures up the opposite – a small, customerserving firm. But perhaps not – perhaps it suggests aggressive selling, deceptive advertising, and wasteful duplication. Those are interesting issues, but thinking about the ideas of competition and monopoly also leads to some important insights in economics and economic development more generally.

In this area, textbooks tend to make two assumptions I want to avoid. One is that each particular industry is more or less destined, because of its characteristics, to be either monopolistic or competitive (or perhaps something else). The second is that competition is somehow the norm and monopoly, if not actually a pathology, is at least unusual. My view is that it is most unusual for any industry to be very clearly of one form or the other – indeed, it is a rare case where it is even worth asking the question. Rather, we have two tools of analysis, two models, two metaphors, with which to understand the world. The task is to put them to work.

Monopoly

In thinking about these things, we could start with a model of a producer of a good, seeking to sell it for profit. The producer will be confronted with a demand curve of the kind described in chapter 1. We can suppose that it is downward sloping so that lower prices are always associated with greater demand. But except for that fact, there is no reason to expect any particular shape or any particular gradient. In diagram 3 it is drawn as a straight line for no reason except that it is easier to draw that way. From the point of view of the producer – the 'firm' as economists always say – the demand curve depicts the options it has for price and quantity combinations. If the firm chooses to set price at p_1, it will sell q_1; if it chooses p_2, it will sell q_2. It is perhaps worth noting that we could equally say that if it decides to sell q_1, it will be able to achieve price p_1; if q_2, then p_2. The real point is not to worry about whether the firm chooses price or chooses quantity, but to see the demand curve as depicting its choices amongst price–quantity combinations.

This producer is in effect what the textbooks call a 'monopolist'. There, the idea is that there is only one producer of the product in question. That raises the same question as appeared in Box 4 as to what counts as 'a product'. Rather than be distracted by that, I would say that the practical implication of the idea of 'monopoly' is that the analysis proceeds on the basis that we can ignore the issue of interactions between producers. We are simply considering a firm facing a downward-sloping demand curve, and that is all there is to it.

Here, there is an important point which involves the ever-present and notorious assumption 'other things being equal'. The idea of the demand curve is that it depicts price–quantity combinations available to the firm in given conditions. It is, of course, true that the price–quantity combinations available to an umbrella seller will vary according to the weather; the same is true of everything else when fashions change, or when a consumer boycott starts up because of adverse publicity about the ethics of a producer, or whatever it may be. These things would all be represented as shifts of the demand curve. An outward shift – from D_1 to D_2 in diagram 4 – shows an increase

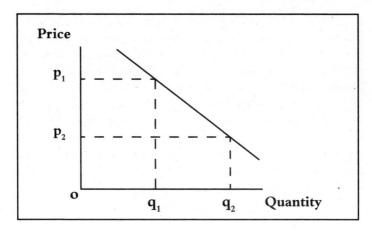

Diagram 3 Demand curve for a 'monopolist'

in demand at each price, and an inward shift would show the opposite. Such things are important, but the point is that, given that all the relevant considerations have been brought to bear, there will be some demand curve, and, until conditions change, that is the one that is relevant to the firm's decisions about price and quantity.

In considering the problem of making the largest possible profit, there may be a temptation to look for the point where revenue – price times quantity – is maximized, but that is a mistake since revenue is not profit. Profit will be what is left of the revenue when costs are deducted. Diagrams 3 and 4 give no indication of the costs. Nevertheless, revenue is relevant and there is a useful trick in what follows, which is to consider the idea of the marginal revenue arising from changes in production. If we think of the firm producing at q_1 on the demand curve in diagram 5, we can ask what change in revenue would arise from an increase in output of one unit. Here there is a trap since we might initially think that, if it is initially producing q_1 and price

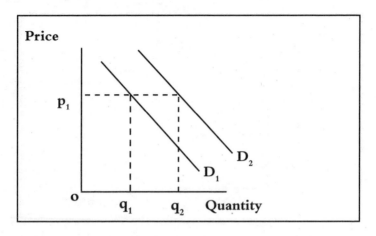

Diagram 4 A shift in demand

p_1 and then produces an extra unit, it earns extra revenue of p_1. Indeed, from the point of view of someone actually performing a sale, that is right – each customer pays the price and an extra customer means extra revenue of that amount. This, however, is a case where the appearance of common sense and the economic analysis are different. The fact that the demand curve is downward sloping means that increased sales are associated with lower prices. The conditions might change – if a more effective sales technique, or a better sales person are found, then it may be possible to sell more at the same price. But if we have found a better sales technique, we have shifted the demand curve – as in diagram 4. If those sorts of conditions stay the same, and the demand curve is downward sloping, extra sales come only with lower prices.

So, looking at diagram 5, if the firm is initially selling q_1 units at price p_1, and it wishes to sell q_2 units, then – on the assumption that all buyers pay the same price – it must charge

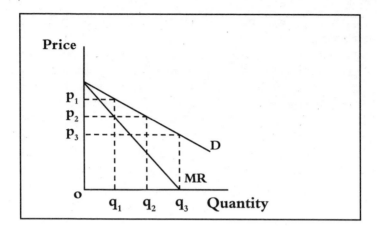

Diagram 5 Demand and marginal revenue

all customers a price of p_2. The change in revenue is then the extra revenue arising from selling extra units at price p_2, *minus* the reduction in revenue on q_1 units which are not being sold for p_1, but for the lower price p_2. A simple example is this: if one unit can be sold for a price of $100, but at a price of $99 there are two buyers, then the marginal revenue of the second sale is the $99 for which it is sold, minus the $1 that has to be cut from the price of the first unit – so the price is $99, but marginal revenue is $98. Another way of looking at it is to say that the total revenue from selling one unit is $100, and from two is $198. Marginal revenue is the extra from selling the second – $98.

A key consequence of that line of reasoning is that at any quantity, marginal revenue will be less than price. That is to say, if an extra item is sold, total revenue will rise by less than the selling price of that extra item. So we can draw a 'marginal revenue curve' along with the demand curve, as in diagram 5, and be sure that the marginal revenue curve will always be below the demand curve.

As it is drawn in diagram 5, marginal revenue is zero when quantity reaches q_3. That simply means that if it were already selling q_3 units, the firm could increase sales by lowering price, but the revenue from the extra sale would be exactly offset by the reduction in the selling price of each of those first q_3 units. It should be recalled here that *price* is not zero; the price at which q_3 units are sold is the price indicated by the demand curve for that quantity – p_3. But the marginal revenue is zero – the firm earns no more by selling more bearing in mind the price reduction that requires. Selling even more units would result in a negative marginal revenue – that is, total revenue would fall. Such outcomes are not usually relevant to business decisions, so we ignore them (and they are not shown in the diagram).

Still this does not tell us anything about the firm's costs, and we need to address that to determine its profit-maximizing quantity. One way of addressing that would be to think about the *total costs* of the firm for different levels of output. Then profit would be the total revenue minus total cost. That will certainly tell us how much profit a firm makes at any level of output, but it is often not the most helpful way of thinking about the question of what level of output will maximize profit.

In the same way that we think of the marginal revenue curve, we can also think of a marginal cost curve. That shows the incremental costs associated with increasing output. That raises the question of how costs change as output increases. One way to think of it would be that, for any particular business, there are certain costs which are unavoidable if the business is to operate. They are its 'fixed' costs. It is as if any firm has to have a health and safety department, and a driver for the managing director – neither of those depends on the level of output. Then there are further costs associated with the output, and which depend on how much is produced. These are sometimes called the 'variable' costs. These are the costs of the labour and materials to actually produce whatever it is they make. A straightforward and reasonably natural way of thinking about it would be to say that the firm has certain fixed costs, and an additional variable cost per unit of output, and that that variable cost gradually increases as output rises – so increasing output becomes more costly at higher levels of output.

These assumptions make it possible to give a clear diagrammatic account of profit maximization which is very much like the discussion of labour demand in chapter 2. It is illustrated in diagram 6. That shows demand and marginal revenue curves like those in diagram 5, along with an upward–sloping marginal cost curve. The quantity that maximizes profit is that where marginal cost and marginal revenue are equal – that is to say, where the marginal revenue and marginal costs curves cross. That this is the correct answer is apparent from this argument: if marginal

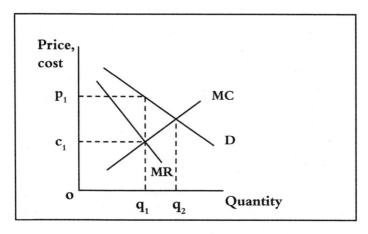

Diagram 6 Demand, marginal revenue, and marginal cost

revenue is greater than marginal cost, increasing output results in more extra revenue than extra cost, and therefore increases profit. On the other hand, if marginal cost is greater than marginal revenue, reducing output saves more in reduced costs than it loses in revenue, and that also increases profit. Only at that mid point where the two are equal is there no such opportunity for profit increase.

We can then also say what the profit-maximizing price is. Since we know the quantity, we can read from the demand curve the price for which this amount can be sold. So the firm – if maximizing profit – produces q_1 and sells it for p_1.

To see how great that profit is, we can then consider the average cost of production – that is, the cost per unit of output (or total cost divided by quantity produced). That obviously depends on both the fixed and variable costs. On the assumptions that have been made, a curve showing average cost will be roughly 'u' shaped. This reflects the ideas that there are some fixed costs (health and safety, MD's driver), so that the per-unit cost of producing a small amount of output is high. As output rises, these sorts of costs are spread over a larger quantity of output so that the average cost of producing a larger amount is lower. On the other hand, at high levels of output, rising variable costs predominate over the effect of spreading the fixed cost, so that average (or 'per-unit') costs again rise. Profit can then be visualized as the shaded area in diagram 7. That shows the price times the quantity, which is total revenue, minus the average cost times the quantity, which of course is total cost. So it shows total revenue minus total cost, which is profit.

There is, of course, nothing forcing the firm to maximize profit (unless the maximum profit achievable is zero). Alternatives might be a careless attitude to customer relations or lax cost control, for example. Simply ignoring the phone is an alternative to maximizing profit, as is appointing incompetent family members to senior positions. Or, for that matter, engaging in

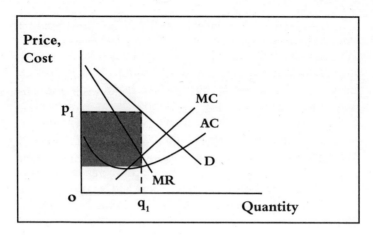

Diagram 7 Profit

activities exhibiting 'corporate social responsibility' may reduce profit, but nevertheless be thought desirable.

So far so good. That is an economic model. It is not a refined model, and it has plenty of clear limitations and various little gaps in the logic. Never mind. As with the earlier discussion of the used–car market, the question is whether the model provides useful insight and, as usual, the best thing is to carry on and find out.

Amongst the insights arising from considering this model, first of all there is the point that profit maximization arises where marginal cost is the same as marginal revenue. That point is much more general than the model, of course, and comes up, with slight variations, again and again in economics. Another point is that profit-maximizing price is always higher than marginal cost. In diagram 6 that is apparent from the fact that the demand curve is always above the marginal revenue curve. The *quantity* to be sold is determined by the intersection of MC and MR – that is, q_1 in diagram 6. But there, *marginal cost* is c_1, so quantity is q_1 and the *price* at which that quantity can be sold is p_1. That is important because it has the unfortunate consequence that there are consumers who would be willing to pay a price which is greater than the marginal cost of production – c_1 – but less than p_1 who end up not buying the product. In that sense there is a way in which the system has failed – both the consumer and the producer could be made better off if there were extra production up to q_2, with the extra units of output sold for prices between the marginal cost of that unit and the maximum a consumer would be willing to pay for it. The model therefore exhibits a basic inefficiency in that the arrangement fails to deliver technically achievable outcomes desired by all concerned. One view of that is that it shows the limitations of the argument considered on pages 25 to 27 and 36 to 37 to the effect that, in the market system, the desires of consumers drive the allocation of productive resources. That does happen, but in circumstances like those under discussion here, the effect is less than perfect – there are some consumers who would be happy to pay the cost of hiring more resources to produce the good in question.

THE MARGIN

The idea of the margin is important in all kinds of economic analysis because it sets the amount of something that someone wants, or the number of times something will be done, or something of that kind. The 'marginal product of labour' is one important case, but we can equally well consider the marginal benefit of eating sausages. So long as that becomes smaller and smaller as someone eats more sausages, then there will be some sausage which is only just worth its price. That determines the number of sausages that person buys.

The idea of the margin is of particular importance in recognizing how price changes affect decisions. It is sometimes easy to feel, for example, that small changes in prices would have no effect on

THE MARGIN (*cont.*)

behaviour. Who, it is sometimes asked, would import Greek, rather than German goods, just because there was a small fall in the price of the Greek ones? There is an illusion there because of the temptation to think of an average buyer of average German goods. *That* person very possibly would be unaffected. But there is, as it were, *someone* just on the edge of wanting to try Greek wine for the first time who *can* be induced to do so by a small price change. That person is the marginal consumer, and it is the existence of some people in that position that makes the operation of the price system effective – the fact that most people are not at the margin is an irrelevance.

Here is something else we might take from the model, which is a bit more surprising. That is, that if some authority – the government presumably – were to legislate a *maximum* price the firm was allowed to charge, this could lead to its producing and selling more. Consider a price like p_2 in diagram 8 – it is below

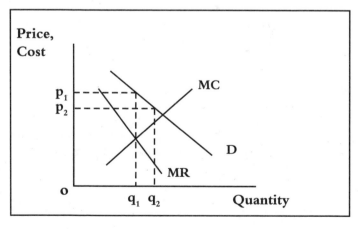

Diagram 8 Illustrating the effect of a legislated maximum price

the profit-maximizing price of p_1. If the firm has to charge p_2, then p_2 is also its marginal revenue for any quantity up to q_2 and the point where marginal revenue is the same as marginal cost is therefore to the right of q_1. We would not normally think of forcing a firm to lower its price as being something that would lead it to sell more, but this is such a case.

The reason this happens is evident from thinking more about the idea of the marginal revenue curve. The unregulated firm was led to set output where marginal cost was equal to marginal revenue. Since marginal revenue was downward sloping, that meant that higher sales could only be achieved with a lower price for all the units of the good it was selling. But once it in any case faces a maximum price, it is limited to that lower price. Then, its profit will be lower, but its profit maximizing level of sales will be higher.

So, I have suggested some conclusions arising from the model. Certainly not all of them would have been obvious without it, but they all follow from thinking about the argument constructed around diagram 6. I also want to emphasize that none of them depends critically on assumptions of such things as the demand curve being a straight line. The model was illustrative, and with the illustration we can see these conclusions follow. And, at the same time, we can at least have a good idea of the variations of the model that would have no profound effect on those arguments.

On the other hand, some variations will matter. If we consider a firm that is not maximizing profit, but is intent on growing, subject only to not making a loss, then the story would be different. Some of the same results might arise, but we would have to work it out. But that is only to say that the model does not cover every case. What we have is a good deal of insight about what happens when producers who face downward-sloping demand curves more or less try to maximize profit.

Competition and the sustainability of monopoly

One obviously serious limitation of that analysis is that I have excluded consideration of the effects of the behaviour of other firms. That must matter because, for example, decisions other firms take about prices – particularly when they are producing a similar product – will affect the demand curve drawn above. Furthermore, if the firm is making a profit, it is very natural to suppose that others will seek to imitate its product so as to take a share of those profits. Again, that must be important in a fuller understanding of the market.

So, let us suppose that a second firm sets up, producing a product which imitates that of the first. We can assume that it produces something similar, but not exactly the same – almost as if it was producing the same thing but in a different colour, so that some consumers prefer one, some the other, or perhaps consumers like to buy both kinds. And to avoid complicating the matter, we can assume the second firm is identical to the first in the sense that its costs of production are the same and it also seeks to maximize profit. The model, it might be said, is 'symmetrical' in the sense that the two firms, looking at each other, are in an identical position, so that it is then natural to suppose that the two firms charge the same price.

Then it should be clear that whatever that price is, the first firm will end up selling less than it did when it was the only firm in the market. In other words, at any given price, some of its consumers will have switched to the new firm. There is more to it than that, though, since the idea that the only effect of the appearance of the second firm is to shift the firm 1 demand curve to the left is unsatisfactory. The reason is that its slope should probably change as well – it is natural to think of the first firm's demand curve becoming flatter ('more elastic') as well as moving to the left. We can again address this by thinking of the question as being about how firm 1 determines its profit-maximizing price and quantity both before and after the entry of the second firm. This time, however, we are comparing the effect of changes in its price in the case where firm 1 is the only firm, with the effect of the same changes in its price when firm 2 is present, but keeps its price unchanged.

Consider the case where price is initially set at the profit-maximizing level, and we ask what would happen to the quantity sold if firm 1 were to increase price by a certain amount – say five percent. In the case where firm 1 is the only producer, a price increase will certainly reduce sales, but here the consumers have no other producer of a similar product to go to – so they are consuming less. In the case where firm 2 is present, the natural presumption is that a five-percent price increase by firm 1 will cost it *more* sales. That is because customers have the option of buying a similar product from firm 2. In that case, the effect of the entry of firm 2 is to move firm 1's demand curve to the left and to make it 'more elastic' (that is, flatter).

It might seem that we learned the not terribly surprising fact that the appearance of a competitor firm reduces the profits of the first one. We have, but there is more to it than that. The *profit margin* has fallen as well: the price being charged is closer to marginal cost than it was. The firm does not welcome that, but from the consumers' point of view it is good news. More than that, it also means that price is nearer to marginal cost, so the price paid by consumers better reflects the actual costs of production. Consequently, the inefficiency of the system is reduced.

Having come that far it should be clear that there is the possibility of a third and a fourth firm appearing as well. Working on the basis that the inducement to set up with a rival product arises from the fact that the existing firms are profit-making, then all the while profits remain, the entry of further firms is to be expected. Consequently, a way of looking at the issue is to ask what would have to happen for profit to fall to zero. (In economics, 'profit' is the revenue in excess of the minimum required to keep the firm in business. So, a firm making 'zero profit' is one for which the accounting profit is just enough for the owners to stay in that business rather than switching to another, taking employment in the factory down the road, retiring, or whatever.)

To answer that question, we again refer to the average cost curve, as illustrated in diagram 9, just as it was in diagram 7 – thinking of diagram 9 as representing the situation of a single, typical firm. We can apply the argument already made about the entry of the second firm, and think of more and more firms entering. With each one that enters, the demand curve for those already existing shifts to the left and becomes more nearly horizontal. At some point it will therefore be just touching the average cost curve. Then, if the firm produces the price and quantity indicated by that point where they touch, its average cost is equal to its price and so profit is zero. And we can see that zero is then the maximum profit the firm can make since at all other points on the demand curve, average cost is greater than price. At this point the firm maximizes profit, but profit is zero. So, remembering that profit is the excess over what is required to keep the firm in business, we can say that further firms will enter the industry until the demand curve of a typical firm has moved so far to the left, or become so nearly horizontal, that it just touches the typical firm's average cost curve. There is an interesting question as to how nearly horizontal that demand curve is. One possibility – illustrated by D_1 – is that this point occurs on the left-hand side of the average cost curve; another – although it is an extreme case – is that it occurs at point B, where the demand curve, illustrated by D_2, has actually become horizontal.

We could treat that as the end of the story and say that we have discovered another idea of equilibrium in this industry.

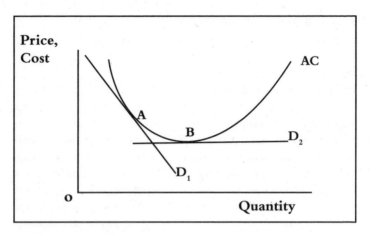

Diagram 9 Entry eliminates profit

We considered the profit-maximizing behaviour of a single firm on the basis that there were no relevant concerns about the behaviour of any competitors. If that is the basis on which we are working, that is a perfectly serious answer. But, alternatively, if the appearance of other firms is a possibility, 'equilibrium' has a different meaning – the entry of additional firms into the industry drives profit to zero. The difference between the two is entirely a matter of what question we are asking.

Perfect competition

We could take this argument to one particular extreme and consider the case where the firm's demand curve actually becomes horizontal when it just touches the average cost curve. That would be the situation in diagram 9 if the demand curve touched the average cost curve at point B. This is a 'perfectly elastic' demand curve. This is a natural view of the case where the buyers regard one firm's product as identical to another's. In that case the buyers have no reason to do anything but buy at the lowest price. And, for that reason, any producer trying to sell at a higher price than others will sell nothing – hence the demand curve the firm faces is horizontal.

Although that outcome is an extreme case, it is one worth pondering as it features in a great deal of economic theory. It corresponds to what is known as 'perfect competition'. As it is usually described in textbooks, perfect competition prevails when a large number of sellers are producing an identical good in conditions where there are neither economies of scale nor barriers to entry of new firms or exit of existing ones. In this case, not only is profit zero, but the size of each firm is optimized in the sense that output is at the point of minimum average cost.

That idea of perfect competition is an important one for a couple of reasons of quite different sorts. Firstly, if it ever arises, it is in certain respects a highly desirable outcome. One reason for this is that the costs of production across the whole industry are minimized – there is no room for incompetent relatives here, since the maximum profit attainable is zero. Secondly, consumers pay the actual cost of production. At point B, the price is equal to the cost of production and, unlike the cases considered so far, everyone willing to pay that cost – and no more – purchases the good. That is an important sense in which the perfectly competitive delivers a desirable outcome. A theorist's delight in economics is imagining the world where every industry is perfectly competitive so that the whole system is efficient. It is a kind of nirvana of consumer sovereignty – although entirely theoretical.

Another point that makes the theory of perfect competition important is that it forms the setting of a large number of other arguments. I shall consider some in later chapters, but the recurring point is that it is often assumed – albeit sometimes implicitly – that perfect competition prevails, as it were, in the background of whatever argument is being made. So it is important simply in terms of helping to understand what economists are on about. Whether or not it is sensible to do so, they are often assuming perfect competition offers a reasonable description of economic organization.

Perfect competition or monopoly?

So here we have two models: monopoly and competition. Students are too often led to suppose that some industries are competitive and others monopolistic and others somewhere in between, and that the most interesting thing we can do is list examples of each. We might think of Microsoft at the height of the popularity of Windows as being the 'sole producer' of a product, and hence a monopoly. Coffee shops in large cities would be an example of perfect competitors. I suppose it is immediately apparent that there are a very large number of intermediate cases. If we think of supermarkets or airlines, it is certainly not right to say there is only one, but it is not quite right to say there is a very large number, and there is also the complicating factor that the product offered is usually not quite the same. Virgin Atlantic and British Airways do offer transatlantic flights, and some people regard them as the same. But, on the other hand, many people seem to have a strong preference for one or the other. Once we reach that point, of course, we might say that Microsoft never was exactly the 'only' producer of operating systems, and nor do all the coffee shops produce exactly the same thing. With that thought we could well question whether there are any interesting cases of true monopolies or perfect competitors at all.

So, if we take it literally, all the examples turn out to be somewhere in between, and it starts to seem as if we have wasted time considering two models neither of which describes anything that exists. But that is not the point at all. Neither case has much reality but they each describe a limiting case of what would happen if certain forces were able to pull hard enough. Taken together they suggest a dynamic system of tension created by the profit motive. On the one hand, any firm can expect to be able to make a profit or increase its profit if it can either lower its costs, or shift its demand curve to the right, or make it less elastic (more nearly vertical). On the other hand, if it is making a profit – and the more so if it is making a large one – it can expect to attract imitators, and the appearance of those imitators tends to shift its demand curve to the left and usually to make it more nearly horizontal – or more 'elastic'. So there is a constant tension between the two extremes.

The drive to lower costs is universal for a profit-seeking firm. To the extent that 'lower costs' means 'fewer resources consumed in the process of production' it is entirely desirable that it should be. To shift its demand curve, the firm must find something to make its product more attractive. That is an incentive to innovate. That innovation might be no more than the same goods being more attractively packaged or more intensively advertised. But it might be the creation of really new goods, or genuine improvements in the quality of existing goods, offering consumers something they value that was not available before. Those who create the goods may well make a profit out of doing so, but the benefit to consumers is real. Indeed they are the substance of economic and material progress (and probably not irrelevant to cultural progress either).

So we might have innovation as banal as different music in the barber shop; or as tacky as repetitive TV advertisements for the latest device for slicing onions – 'But wait, that's not all. Order now and we'll give you two for the price of one!' Or it could be as superficial as the latest piece of guile to make it seem we can never appear amongst our friends without the right wrist watch. Or it could be the home computer or iTunes. Or it could be domestic refrigeration – think what a difference that makes to the quality of life in tropical zones. Or it could be a new drug which really does save lives. Whatever the case, in the free market system, successful innovation brings two things: profit and imitators. To the extent that the development of such products results in the developers making a profit, that is partly the inducement for them to innovate, but those profits are also the source of their own undoing. As well as the reward for the innovator, they are lure for the imitators.

All in all, then, we have innovation pulling us towards the pole of the single producer, and imitation pulling us towards perfect competition. The system we observe around us is neither one nor the other – nor would it be, even if it were altogether unregulated. What we observe is the outcome of the tension between the two. The value of the models, then, is nothing whatever to do with leading us to list cases of firms or industries that are one type or the other – or 'approximately' one type or the other. Their value lies in the appreciation they engender of that system as a whole. Interestingly, and most importantly, at both ends of that tension – the pull of innovation, and the pull of imitation – it is, like it or not, the profit motive that does the pulling.

4

Market failure

So, the price system and the profit motive are certainly important, and powerful. But it is widely observed that they can often lead to some very undesirable results as well. The most widely reported is surely the excesses of environmental damage all too clearly resulting from the pursuit of profit. But there are others. As far as economics is concerned, these sorts of things are 'market failures' – cases where, for understandable and perhaps remediable reasons, the price system delivers less than optimal results.

Before considering specific cases of market failure, we should note that the definition of market failure in one way casts the net very wide, while in another it keeps the range of enquiry very narrow. The narrowness comes from the idea of optimality which is at work. Two near-enough equivalent ways of thinking of it are that the market has failed to deliver optimality when the price of goods or services is not equal to their marginal cost; or alternatively that there are unrealized, potential transactions which could make both parties better off. As that makes clear, no issues of moral worth, equality, or fairness are raised. Those factors are not the idea of 'market failure' at all.

The breadth comes from the wide range of issues which can be seen to fit this definition. Two examples have already come up. The discussion of the problem in the used-car market was one. The other was in the discussion of 'monopoly' – or generally of the firm with a downward-sloping demand curve. Indeed, both of these feature routinely on textbook lists of market failure, and the cases like the used cars do so uncontroversially.

Monopoly as a market failure

The case of monopoly is more peculiar. If there is the kind of relation between monopoly and innovation described in chapter 3 – so that the creation of temporary monopoly is the consequence of innovation, and monopoly profit the inducement for it – it seems strange to regard it as a failure of the market. One thought is that there might be other sources of innovation, but still it is hard to escape the view that there is some link between it and monopoly. Indeed, through the granting of patents, policymakers create or protect monopoly. The reason is that many ideas protected by patents would otherwise be too easy to imitate, and profits from the innovations would be too short-lived to induce the investment required to make them. An often-cited example is that of the development of new medical drugs. It is partly a hit-and-miss process, requiring expensive experimentation, but when a new drug is devised, it is usually easy to copy. The making of chemically identical copies would put its production into near-perfect competition, making it impossible to recoup the expenses of the experimentation. That means there would be no profit to be made in undertaking the experiments in the first place. One response might be to nationalize the research, so that it would not be undertaken by profit-making firms, but if private enterprise is to engage in such research, it is easy to see why some kind of patent system is regarded as important.

So what should we say about labelling things as 'failures' whilst deliberately creating them? Part of the answer is that the terminology arises from the emphasis that is put on the theoretical analysis of very long-run equilibrium. The vision is that, in the longest of long runs, all opportunities for innovation are exhausted. Innovation, we might say, has no place there – it is strictly an aspect of disequilibrium. That may not be a satisfactory response, but in any case, the rest of the answer is simply that the terminology *is* rather peculiar. That does no real harm – we can perfectly well understand the sense in which the existence of monopoly prevents mutually beneficial trades occurring; but the possibility of monopoly speeds innovation, so that, all things considered, it is better, sometimes, to permit or even create it.

That is not the whole story as far as monopoly-as-market-failure is concerned. There are various other ways in which the theoretical idea of a monopoly is either part of a further important thought about market failure, or can readily be developed into one. One is that the pricing behaviour of a monopolist might be imitated by a group of firms forming a cartel, or price-fixing agreement. Whilst such cartels persist, they can certainly raise price above what it would otherwise be, but there are two potentially important limitations on their power. The first arises as a so-called 'prisoner's dilemma' with respect to each other.

The original prisoner's dilemma, after which the idea is named, is not really something with any direct application to economics, but the ideas underlying it are applicable to a number of circumstances. We can first consider an industry where there are two producers who might form a cartel. If they do, they can raise price above what it would otherwise be, but they are constrained by the demand curve, so they can raise price only by restricting output. We can assume that each aims to maximize profit and, to be clear, this means they are interested in achieving maximum profit for themselves, not in benefiting or harming the other, nor in the outcome in terms of their profit relative to that of the other. These simple souls are just trying to make as much money as they can for themselves.

Then, from the point of view of firm A, firm B will either conform to the cartel agreement and restrict output, or it will not. We assume that if firm B is breaking the agreement it means that the price will in any case be low, and that in this case firm A makes the greatest profit by also breaking the agreement. On the other hand, if B conforms to the agreement, then we assume that A's profits are highest by breaking the agreement and taking advantage of the price rise created by B's restricting output. If that is how things are, A's profit–maximizing strategy is always to break the agreement no matter what B does. If that is all there is to it, that is what A will do. B, of course, is in the same position – it is another symmetrical model – and thus also breaks the agreement. This outcome is characteristic of the prisoner's dilemma: there is an agreement available which, if adhered to, makes both participants better off than if they both break it; yet both are led to break it by the fact that whatever the other does, breaking it is the best option for them individually.

GAME THEORY

'Game theory' used to be regarded as a specialization within economics, with the 'prisoner's dilemma' being its emblem. It was thought of as the part of economics that was concerned with analysing strictly rational behaviour. Since then, the centre of gravity of economics has moved away from its concern with historical development, institutional structures, and appreciation of social motivations. It has become much more about rational action.

Now, the prisoner's dilemma – in one form or another – is part of everybody's idea of what modern economics is about. But much of the rest of economics could be called game theory as well. So, the education signalling model, to be discussed shortly, is a kind of game between the students and the employer; the used-car problem is a kind of game between buyers and sellers. The problem faced by the workers who would like to commit to not going on strike if an investment in new machinery is made, but cannot make that promise credible, would certainly be called 'game theory' by many. So, from the point of view of appreciating what economics is all about, there is no point in considering game theory separately. In so far as there continues to be a specialization of game theory within economics it is mainly concerned with abstruse ramifications of various games with, most of the time, much more interest in sophisticated mathematics than the applicability of the ideas to any practical problem.

The argument can be extended to more than two participants. If there are several potential members of a cartel, exactly
the same sort of thing happens. Each one can see that, if the price
is raised by the restriction of the output of others or some of
them, then they are best off riding that increase by cutting their
own price and selling a large amount, and if the others do not
restrict output, so that price will not be high in any case, it only
harms them to restrict their own output.

There are various other possibilities, of course – the participants play golf together and are good friends; they are afraid of
having their legs broken if they fail to abide by the agreement;
or perhaps they are in a long-term cartel relationship where
the value of keeping it going is worth giving up the immediate benefits of breaking it. Still, even in these sorts of cases, the
argument described above does create an incentive to break
the agreement and suggests that cartels may have a tendency
to be unstable. (In many contexts they are illegal, as well, and
in some places prosecutors take a lenient view of the first firm
to report the existence of a cartel – that must make them even
less stable.)

The second problem for a cartel is that of restricting entry. A
successful cartel, after all, makes profit in just the way a monopoly does. It thereby creates an inducement for other producers
to enter the industry. It is not an entirely straightforward matter
because if entry causes the cartel to break up, it may destroy
the basis for the profitability of entry itself. Business life has
such hazards, but clearly the incentive to enter the industry of a
successful cartel may be present, and that cannot make the main-
tenance of the cartel any easier.

There is one particularly interesting way of addressing the
problem of the instability of cartels. When a group of suppliers
are able either to regulate entry to their business, or induce the
government to do so, they acquire some of the benefits of a cartel,
but quite legally. Consider, for example, the case of licensed

professionals, an interesting thought because such arrangements are invariably advocated on the basis of the benefits they bring to consumers, in terms of guaranteed quality and the like. Yet the clearly apparent benefit is to the producers, who are protected from competition from 'unlicensed' providers. Quality may or may not be guaranteed, but to the extent that price is raised, some would-be consumers end up going without the service altogether.

So, what of the thought that a free market in medical care would allow anyone to sell their product? Most people react to such ideas with astonishment and horror. The first thought is that it would allow quacks to take large amounts of money from people for doing nothing useful and perhaps much that was harmful. Maybe it would, but that is certainly not the *whole* answer. The trick to seeing merit in such proposals – or for people who do not idolize the market to see such merit – is to think how the incentives of rational agents would guide behaviour in such a system. One point is that those seeking medical services would have every reason to check up on the providers. Consequently, those offering them would certainly value their reputations. That might, for example, lead individual providers to join together in offering a 'branded product' and themselves certifying the competence of their members. There are many other possibilities along those lines, illustrating the point, amongst others, that *state* licensing is far from the only way of guaranteeing quality, and whether it is the best one is then the next question.

The medical case is obviously an extreme one. What about lawyers? Or what about barbers and piano teachers? I understand licences have been required for both of those in some places. Can those learning the piano and their parents really not find out which teachers are any good without someone from the government telling them? Well, what about people who write introductory books on economics, then? If there are going to be state licences for any of these products, and it is a fair bet that there are, it is an interesting problem to decide what should determine where the boundary is.

But some points we can make. One is that the existing producers, those with the licences or who will easily get one if they are introduced, certainly have reason to favour the scheme, and other would-be producers to reject it. Another is perhaps that, if we are interested in understanding the forces leading to the introduction of such things, the interests of producers should be scrutinized at least as much as the interests of consumers.

Another situation worthy of special attention is that of 'natural monopoly'. That is a situation in which the technology of production is such that the average cost of production falls as output rises over the whole relevant range of production. In the most extreme case, having two producers in the world would make cost per unit of output appreciably higher than if there is only one. It is sometimes said this is true of Boeing and Airbus, with the two of them only coexisting because of government subsidies. But at the other extreme, there could perfectly well be a village pub which is a 'natural monopoly'. If there were two pubs, neither could be large enough to operate at an efficient scale. The result would be that if it turned out to be possible for two pubs to stay in business at all, they could do so only as high-cost pubs, which therefore would charge consumers high prices. Even though there would be an element of competition, the overall effect might be to make prices paid by consumers higher with two pubs than with just one.

A related case where the power of imitation to erode monopoly is severely constrained arises from the fact that – in one way or another – the important thing for the consumers is not to have the best or most suitable or best-value product but, rather, as it were, to have the same one as everyone else. One example would be the position of eBay. There would no doubt be some expenses in setting up in competition with eBay, but they can hardly be so great that in themselves they prevent others entering the industry. A greater difficulty may be that both buyers and sellers are generally better off going to whichever site has the largest number of participants. So, even if someone were to design such a site which, in technical and user-friendliness terms, was plainly and unarguably better than eBay, it might be difficult to attract large numbers of users. So in this kind of case, again, there is no guarantee of the free market delivering what consumers really want. There is plenty of scope for market failure.

'Moral hazard' and its family

One problem of determining the quality of goods for sale has already been considered. In chapter 1, the asymmetry of information between buyer and seller gave rise to the possibility that the market for high-quality goods – cars, in the example I used – would be impaired, and mutually beneficial trades not be made. Fundamentally, the problem was the asymmetry of information, combined with the fact that everyone knew there was an asymmetry of information. The sellers of good cars knew their cars were good, but their difficulty was persuading the potential buyers of that fact. That case is sometimes called one of 'adverse selection'.

I promised more of that general type, and one large group concerns a problem known to economists as that of 'moral hazard'. Like adverse selection, true cases of moral hazard arise from asymmetric information. In this case, the problem is that some arrangement might be made which would potentially be beneficial to two parties, but it is not possible for each party to observe the behaviour of the other, and one of them has incentives not to keep the agreement. Since those incentives are understood by both parties from the beginning, no agreement is actually made. (Or an agreement is made, but it does not go as far as it would with better information.)

Consider two agents, A and B. A does no work but owns facilities, equipment, or the like which can be used by B to produce a good or service for sale. We can consider three kinds of arrangement that they might make. One would be for A to be paid a fixed amount – a rental fee, in effect – for the equipment, and B to keep the other earnings of the business. In the second, B is paid a fixed fee – it would be like a wage – and A keeps the rest. The third case would be a sharing scheme, and to keep it simple we can think of the case where the whole proceeds are simply split 50-50. In addition, mixtures of these are possible, so that, say, A or B receives some fixed payment, and some share of the residual proceeds.

To cast this as a problem of asymmetric information, we can assume that the amount of the good that is eventually produced depends on two things – the effort of B, and unpredictable matters of luck (the weather, or the business conditions, or whatever it may be) – and that whilst these are both known (after the fact, in the case of the 'luck') to B, they are unobservable to A.

The difficulty with the wage scheme is that B's income is guaranteed by the form of the agreement. So long as making an effort is a cost to B, the result will be that little (or no) effort is made. The result is that, on average, there will be little output. B still receives the wage, but A receives little (or nothing). There is a market failure in that B would be willing to work harder to produce more if paid for that extra effort. The marginal cost – which is B's effort – is less than the true value of output that could be made with that effort. This is a pure case of 'moral hazard'.

If B's effort were observable, then the payment of the wage could be made conditional on an appropriate effort – that would provide an incentive for effort. Equally if the 'luck' matters were observable, B's effort could be deduced, and again the wage could be conditional. But in the asymmetric information case under discussion those things are not observable.

There is, however, as the problem has been put so far, a perfectly satisfactory solution. That is to switch to the 'rental' arrangement. That puts B in the position of paying a fixed amount to A, but then keeping all the residual proceeds. B then earns the whole marginal product from marginal effort and will therefore make the effort which (on average, allowing for luck) makes the value of the product equal to the marginal cost of producing it. B's effort is therefore ensured by the fact that all of the *extra* output resulting from it is paid to B. Although I have labelled this a 'rental' scheme, it should be clear that in terms of its outcomes it is very much like an employment contract with a very high degree of performance-related pay. That is because in both cases there is a high degree of translation of the efforts of the employee into extra income.

That solution, however, might not be effective if we think of possible developments of the argument. One would be the case where B is not a person, but a team. If the output of the enterprise depends on the efforts of all team members, but these are not observable to each other, then the workers are in a relation vis-à-vis each other with some resemblance to that of A and B in the original statement. They could collectively pay A a fee for the use of the equipment, and divide the remaining proceeds. But each then receives a portion of those proceeds. Thinking of one of the people – person B1, I suppose – making extra effort results in extra income, but that income is divided between the team.

So, if there are ten people in the team and they all make an extra effort to increase output by 100, they each receive 10 extra. But suppose that if nine make the extra effort and one does not, output is increased by 90. If no one can tell who it was *not* making an effort, we might suppose that in that case each receives an extra 9. So here, B1 was prepared to make the effort for 10 extra units, but will get 9 of them without making an effort. So only 1 extra unit is actually earned by making the effort, and that may not be a sufficient inducement. The same argument applies to all of the team, of course, so – in the extreme case – none of them makes an effort and the increase in output is not achieved. (If, contemplating that outcome, one does make an effort, then that might bring extra output of 10, but, again, it is to be divided between the ten of them, so the effort-maker still only receives 1.)

Perhaps that is too extreme a case, since it supposes that the individuals have no sense of duty to their team, and that their efforts are completely unobservable. But, as usual, arguing for the extreme version of the point is not important – the observation is that the pressures in that kind of situation are to make too little effort.

The argument obviously resembles the 'prisoner's dilemma' from earlier. Indeed, the structure of the problem is very similar, although this one is sometimes described as a 'free rider problem'. In the extreme case the workers have nothing to gain from making an effort. If the others make an effort, they benefit from the 'free ride' this creates. If the others do not make an effort, there is nothing to be done.

An alternative development of the original argument is to consider the case where B, but not A, is 'risk averse'. That is to say that B prefers a certain payment to a random payment which is on average equal to the certain amount. In that case the randomness in the determination of output is relevant not only because it makes it impossible to be sure what effort B made, but because it directly imposes costs. Then, the 'rental' arrangement has the disadvantage, as compared to the 'wage' one, that the risk-averse person carries the risk.

If we were to think only of the risk issue, we would adopt the wage scheme – that puts the whole risk on A; thinking of only the incentive issue, we would adopt the rental scheme. Where both issues are present, the best solution will be somewhere in between. For example, it might be the 50-50 sharing scheme. That gives B both some incentive to work, and some protection against the randomness of the outcomes. The disappointing result is that it does neither completely. There are in a sense two market failures here – B's incentive to provide effort is incomplete; and B would like to be – and would be willing to pay to be – more fully insured against the variability.

That matter of 'insurance' can be considered in its own right – the problem follows that of A and B described above very closely. In this case, B is a person seeking insurance; A is the provider of insurance. The 'effort' of B is to be understood as the effort required to avoid the accident, or whatever it is that is the subject of the insurance; the 'luck' is the unavoidable aspect of risk which provides the basic motivation for seeking insurance. Again we can say that to the extent that taking care is costly to B, having insurance will lead B to take less care. In the extreme case, insurance is so complete that B actually ceases to care whether the accident occurs and makes no effort to avoid it. (In this case the insurance would be covering the direct loss of the accident, and the inconvenience and costs of making the claim, and so on.)

What we learn from this is that B cannot expect to be able to purchase such complete insurance. In other words, even when insured, B will be bearing some risk. However slight that remaining risk, B, being risk-averse, would be willing to pay something to avoid it. Meanwhile, A, not being risk-averse, would be willing to take a payment to provide B with that insurance – but only so long as that arrangement did not itself affect the chance of the accident. There would be no problem if either the care taken by B made no difference to the likelihood of a claim – I suppose that is true in earthquake insurance, for example – or if it were possible, after the event, to ascertain how much care B had taken. The insurance contract would stipulate the required care, and if that was not taken, there would be no payment. B would then have an incentive to take care. But in that case, there would be no relevant asymmetry of information. In the circumstances under discussion, however, there is a market failure in that B would like to buy and A would like to sell insurance, but the transaction cannot be made.

Another related case might be that of the relation of a lender and a borrower – the lender wants the loan used in a way that makes repayment secure. From the borrower's point of view, though, if the loan is not repaid, then the consequences (bankruptcy) are what they are, but being bankrupt for a small amount and being bankrupt for a large amount come to the same thing. On the other hand, large profits made accrue to the borrower. That may make the borrower – contrary to the lender's interests – favour risky uses of the loan. Alternatively, it encourages borrowing for purposes which are intrinsically risky but can be presented to the lender as being safer than they are. In either case, the awareness of all this amongst lenders (or potential lenders) reduces their willingness to lend or leads them to lend only at higher interest rates than they otherwise would. In any case, we again have market failure in that there exist safe projects but the loans for them may not be forthcoming. The reason is again one of asymmetric information: the lenders cannot establish what kind of project will be pursued if the loan is made.

There are any number of similar possible cases. The trick to identifying them is to see the pattern – two agents in a contractual or contract-like relationship, with one required to make some kind of 'effort' which either benefits both agents, or increases the resources that can be divided between them, but the circumstances are such that the effort cannot be precisely observed or measured. One variation has both agents benefiting from the same outcomes, but the costs of the effort falling predominantly on one of them. That is the original case where the issue was between the 'wage' and the 'rental' agreement. In another scenario, the issue of the costs of effort is not to the fore – rather, it is the extent to which each party gains from favourable outcomes. That was the case in the lender/borrower example.

Yet another variation sees the two parties benefiting from distinct but related outcomes. One example might be the issue between the shareholders and managers of a large company. Perhaps the shareholders value profit and nothing else, whereas the managers value profit and the size of the firm – it might be that there is more prestige in running a large, moderately profitable firm than a smaller, very profitable one. If the shareholders cannot accurately observe the decisions the managers take, the same sort of problem arises as in the other cases.

Of all these cases, those relating to employment and employment-like situations may be the most important. Almost no one is truly in the position of having exactly the same objectives as their employer. Few are very closely supervised, and in any case, the supervisors themselves are usually employees, also subject to the same incentives. There are plenty of related cases, even if not strictly those of employment – the relationship of elected representatives to their electors would be one example – where similar issues arise.

In the employment cases one solution suggests itself very strongly to the economist and another may in fact operate rather often. Between the two, I fear, lies an unfortunate gulf. To the economist, the solution might be to pay more. Consider the basic form of this problem – that put in terms of person A and person B on pages 85 to 86. The worker, for whom effort is costly, cannot be closely supervised, and, being risk-averse, is not given an entirely performance-related payment on the

model of the 'rental' scheme considered above. A clear limitation of the argument as it was put is that it supposed that no
supervision of the worker was possible. It might seem that if
some assessment can be made, then, if nothing else, the threat
of dismissal can encourage effort. Indeed it could, but there are
circumstances where that might not be strong enough. Those
circumstances are, as it happens, the ones described in chapter
2 in connection with the marginal product theory of wages.
It was a consequence of that theory – apparently a desirable
consequence of the market system – that there would be no
involuntary unemployment. Well, to the extent that it is true
that there is no involuntary unemployment, it is also true that
the threat of dismissal is no threat at all – a dismissed worker
can find other employment. In a large enough labour market
where no reputation for laziness catches up with them, they do
so at an unchanged wage.

But what about this: if one firm pays the workers more than
the norm, those workers do have an incentive to make sure they
do not lose their jobs. Even if they walk straight into another, it is a
lower-paid one. So workers who are paid *more* than the going rate
have an incentive to keep their job, and if they are even partially
supervised, that gives them an incentive to work properly. Such
devices are sometimes known as paying 'efficiency wages'.

This opens the possibility that different firms might adopt
different strategies – there could be high-pay, low-supervision
firms, and low-pay, high-supervision ones – each making satisfactory profit. The impression might then be created that the
high-paid workers are more capable than the others – but that
would not be the case at all. Or it might seem that there is a kind
of market justice in that they deserve their higher wages because
of their hard work. But that is not right either – it is the higher
wages that come first, and they induce the harder work. Here,
the capabilities of the workers might have nothing to do with the
differential earnings, and their different levels of effort might not

be due to the superior character of some, but rather the contractual environment in which they are employed.

An altogether different sort of response, though, is to say that there are other factors motivating the worker – such as all manner of professional ethics and such things as taking pride in their work. That sort of thought does not feature much in the economist's conception of rational behaviour, but it could well be argued that, as a matter of fact, the threat of dismissal and a calculation about what other jobs would be available are not the only factors that keep people working. That, though, is surely more a characteristic of workers in some professions than in others. But if that is so, it means that in those professions, there is less need to pay higher wages (or offer the possibility of promotion to higher wages, or whatever variation of the idea might be considered). It is in the lines of work where commitment to the activity itself is less of a motivation that higher wages need to be paid to extract effort. So, it is the good-for-nothing, lazy, and self-serving, not the community-spirited, loyal, and diligent, from whom effort is extracted by high payments, and consequently to whom such payments are offered. Although it has often been said that virtue is its own reward, it is less often noted that in the world of asymmetric information, moral hazard, and efficiency wages, this may actually be a law of economics.

Commitment and coordination

All of the cases considered in the last section have an aspect of asymmetric information. Another way of looking at it is to say that the problem arises because it is impossible to enter into a binding commitment to behave in a certain way. In the simplest case, although the agent can make a promise to give high effort (or take care, or whatever), there is normally no way to set things up in advance so as to actually guarantee it. There is nothing that a person can do that will actually force them to keep the promise. If it were possible for them to bind their future selves actually to behave in a certain way, the problem would vanish.

Other problems, similar to those above, but where the difficulty of making a binding commitment arises elsewhere, can be imagined. One possible example also takes the idea of the free rider problem to another stage, as well as considering a different possible aspect of the problem faced by A and B considering the choice of wage and rental systems.

Suppose workers are working in a factory and some new equipment becomes available. If the factory owners purchase it, then worker productivity, output, and revenues will all rise; and suppose that the increase in revenue is sufficient to justify the purchase of the equipment, even allowing for paying extra to the workers. But suppose also that the owners and the workers are tied to each other in the sense that the workers cannot easily be replaced by other workers, perhaps because there are too many of them, or they are members of a strong union. The question is, under what conditions do we expect the upgrade to occur?

The common-sense answer is that the parties can reach a new agreement which will share the benefits of the investment between the workers and the firm. Since by assumption the benefit of that equipment is large enough to more than cover its costs, there will be a range of such agreements – some more beneficial to one, some to the other, but both can certainly benefit. The difficulty is that, once some mutually acceptable arrangement is reached, if the investment is made, the workers are then in a position to renege on the agreement and demand a larger share. The workers can, as we might say, 'go on strike'. At that point, the investment having been made, the firm's bargaining power is weak. In the extreme case, where there really are no alternative uses for the equipment, the workers can take the whole of the extra output. That would be the end of the story, but of course it is not the end of the reasoning process. The reason is that this problem can be recognized in advance so that, if there is a threat of such a strike, the investment will not be made – from the point of view of the owners of the firm it would be better to spend the funds on a party. There is clearly a market failure here since all concerned would be better off if the investment took place and they shared the benefits.

I have described this as a problem of 'commitment' because the workers are in the seemingly peculiar position of being damaged by the inability to give up what appears to be a strength. It is rather like the case of the sellers of good cars being disadvantaged by their knowledge. If these workers could, as it were, throw away the ability to go on strike, they would put themselves in a weaker bargaining position. But in that weaker position they would achieve a better outcome, since then the investment would be made.

That conclusion illustrates the kind of problem, but might not be the end of the matter. Sometimes a simple contract will solve a problem of this kind, but it might be difficult to specify its exact terms. Another sort of solution arises from the fact that many of the interactions in question are repeated so that there is scope for the parties to establish reputations for cooperation, and, having established them, to want to keep them. It is rather like the benefits of branding of high-quality products in an adverse selection situation. If, perhaps, the investment under consideration is only one of a sequence of possible investments, the union will recognize that it gains something from each of them. That gives it reason to cooperate each time one is made. The firm can see that the union has this reason to cooperate and to that extent can be confident that it will. That might be at least a partial solution. We can add, too, that the firm has a similar motive to establish a reputation for undertaking such investments. On the other hand, if the point is ever reached where the firm appears to have made its last investment, at that point the union has no reason to maintain its reputation for cooperation.

That way of looking at the problem perhaps raises the possibility that there could be alternative paths of development. In one there is the required trust between firms and unions, and investment proceeds apace, unions cooperate, and the profits generated make for more investment, with wages rising rapidly as the process continues. In the other, without the trust, investments are infrequent and, when they occur, are not expected to recur, so attract attempts by the unions to extract the largest share they can of the benefits. The comparison of West Germany or Japan with the United Kingdom in the 1960s and 1970s suggests itself. In the first two, industrial investment and modernization seemed to proceed quickly, in an environment of harmonious industrial relations. In the third the opposite seemed to happen and, rather as the argument suggests is to be expected, it was never quite clear whether industrial relations were poor because of poor industrial performance, or industrial performance was poor because of the bad relations. And indeed, on the basis of the analysis suggested, it is neither quite one thing nor quite the other.

We could equally well think of similar cases where the agents take their decisions simultaneously, rather than one after the other. That might result in a prisoner's dilemma of the kind already discussed on pages 79 to 81. But there are related cases. One, with some importance, arises in the context of doubts about the reliability of banks. The basis of the business of the simplest kind of bank is that it takes deposits, which can be withdrawn at short notice, and makes long-term loans. All is well while the loans are sound and there is a steady flow of reasonably predictable deposits and withdrawals. But if the soundness of the loans comes into question, then the bank's ability to pay all its depositors is in question, but those who are *first* to ask for their money can be paid. Consequently all the depositors have an incentive to seek to withdraw their money. The bank certainly cannot meet all those demands from its own resources since it cannot quickly retrieve the money it has lent. The consequence is that in circumstances of such panic, a bank might fail irrespective of whether its loans are in fact sound. That is certainly a market failure.

One response is that the central bank acts as 'lender of last resort', ready to provide emergency loans so that a sound bank can stay in business. There is also the case where the bank is fundamentally unsound, of course – it actually has made bad loans and will have to go out of business. In that case, rather than a lender of last resort, what is required is deposit insurance, and indeed such insurance is commonplace in advanced banking systems.

From the point of view of practical policy, that may be about all there is to it – the lender of last resort and deposit insurance schemes protect the depositors and hence substantially avoid the difficulties caused by them losing confidence in a bank. From the point of view of economic analysis, there is perhaps a distinction to be made between a bank run which is purely a matter of rumour and panic, and one which arises from the rational action of the depositors. In practical terms they may be hard to distinguish, but the depositors do not generally know for sure whether a bank is sound. So, in the uninsured system, any reasonable doubt could well make it rational for them to seek to withdraw their funds. And if others are withdrawing theirs on an unusually large scale, that certainly makes the failure of the bank more likely, so there could be such a thing as a *rational* run on a bank which, except for the occurrence of the run, is quite safe. Again, we find a case where rationality is no guarantee of market effectiveness.

Education and asymmetric information

Adverse selection and moral hazard have already been considered. The bank run problem also had an aspect of asymmetric information. Another related example that has attracted particular attention concerns the value of education. If we consider the position of people with little or no work experience seeking a job, then they are in a similar position to the sellers of untested products, or products with no brand-based reputation. They certainly know more about their own abilities (including such things as their work ethic) than the potential employers do, but they are usually in no position to offer product warranties. In the manner of the used-car problem, then, those who are in fact good, hard workers are at risk of not being able to sell their labour services for an appropriate price.

One suggestion about this is that educational qualifications may have the effect of demonstrating ability and diligence – they are a 'signal' of ability. We can assume that acquiring educational qualifications is costly in terms of time and effort, but these costs are lower for more able and harder-working people than for the less able. We can also assume that employers pay more – but not too much more – to qualified people. In that case, it could be that the able, but not the less able, have an incentive to bear the costs of acquiring the qualification. From their point of view, the extra they will earn covers the costs of the education; but for the less able – who face greater costs – it will not. In that case, the employers are right to pay more for the highly qualified people because they are then hiring the most able.

Three points in particular can be made about this picture. One is that this 'educational signalling' serves as a kind of substitute for building a brand in a context where there would otherwise be asymmetric information as to quality. Secondly, the symptom of the market failure is the over-investment in education that occurs. The qualifications are not being acquired because they actually enhance ability, but merely because they indicate that the person has the ability. Comparing what is happening with what would happen if there were complete information, too many resources are being spent on teaching, examining, and the like, and the students are spending their own time in education when they would otherwise have started work. Thirdly, and the terrifying part for those in my profession, all this is true even if the process of education adds *nothing* to a student's skills. It is not merely that skill acquisition is not the *motive* for education; it is that there might be no skill acquisition. Even then, there could be a motive for acquiring hard-to-achieve qualifications.

Something that may be less clear is this: although it appears that the arrangement works to the detriment of the less able, and the benefit of the more able, that benefit is not certain. The more able can be in a situation where the costs of acquiring the education are greater than the benefits, in the sense that they would be better off if there were no such signal, and everyone was treated as 'average'. They are nevertheless forced to acquire the education, because if they do not they will be treated not as average, but as less able. They have no way, as it were, to opt out, to say to the employers, 'I am not playing that game, please treat me as average.' The reason they cannot do that is basically one of adverse selection. Hypothetically, if such a plan worked, not just the able, but all the less able could adopt it. But it cannot be that all the less able are treated as 'average'.

If that is how things are, then it is a market failure on a grand scale. In that case, the able are led to the acquisition of qualifications which are of no intrinsic value, in circumstances where the cost of acquiring them is greater than the benefit of having them, relative to the case where no such qualifications were available. Fortunately, no one is likely to take seriously the idea that education imparts no useful knowledge and develops no worthwhile skills. Nor is it really true that employers are ever in the position of having no idea which potential employees are best suited. Even if that were true at the time they were hired, it will not remain true for long. So payments can always be adjusted shortly after hiring people.

There is always the possibility, of course, that there are elements of both skill acquisition and signalling in any educational qualification. And they might come in different proportions in different cases. So, for example, higher degrees with no specific relevance to future employment may be the most likely candidates for signalling considerations.

But perhaps it is also worth saying that 'skill acquisition' and 'signalling' are not the only possibilities. They are the ideas that have motivated a great deal of economic research, but the pure love of learning ought to be mentioned, even though – considering the fees to be paid, and loss of earnings involved – it is probably not the main motivation of many young people. But there is still another possibility, although one hardly ever considered. What about the possibility there is over-investment in education for reasons akin to conspicuous consumption? It is not that a person's employer cannot tell his or her ability; it is that friends and acquaintances – and perhaps family too – need to be reassured. 'Educated at Oxford *and* Harvard! Now, isn't *that* something.'

Externalities and public goods

Another collection of market failures go by the name 'externalities and public goods'. They arise when it is in the nature of the production or consumption of a good that some of the costs or benefits fall on or accrue to individuals who are neither buyers nor sellers of the good. One of the most straightforward examples, as well as one of the most important, is that of pollution. The simple model has a firm involved in making something for sale and the production process emitting a pollutant, which is then damaging to individuals who have nothing to do with the production or consumption of the good – it is, as it is put, a 'negative externality'.

That case is immediately intuitive. Plenty of other cases are very similar and can be understood in the same way as 'pollution'. Others are slightly different, but fit the pattern sufficiently closely to be seen as equivalent. One would be the effect of road users in causing congestion and thereby damaging each other. They are all, as it were, simultaneously in the position of being the creator of negative externalities, and their victim. Each driver makes slower progress because there are so many on the road, and at the same time impedes the progress of the others. There are also companion cases where the effect – the 'pollution' – is something beneficial rather than something harmful: we can just as well think of nice smells being emitted as a by-product of another activity – a 'positive externality'.

The idea of a 'public good' – or a 'pure public good' – is that it is a good which has the two characteristics, that one person's consumption does not diminish the availability of the good for other consumers, and that it is impossible to prevent the consumption of it. Taken literally, there is no such thing in the economic world but there are many things – like street lighting and broadcast TV – that are approximations to it. Those things, of course, are very much like goods which create positive externalities, and indeed it is probably just an historical accident that we have ended up with apparently two different ideas, when they could very well be analysed in much the same terms.

In all cases, the essential of the problem is that in the ordinary course of events there is no market for the costs and benefits arising from externalities, so they go unpriced. For that reason, the consumer preferences and the costs of abatement or production cannot influence the quantities produced. And, consequently, it cannot be that there is any market mechanism that secures optimality.

Taking the case of pollution resulting from some industrial process, a way to think about the problem is this. The true costs of production of the product are the private costs – that is, the wage bill, the costs of supplies, rental of land, and all the things usually regarded as costs – and the 'social costs' – that is, the valuation of the harm done by the externality. The free market system takes account only of the private costs. So, for example, in the case where, but for the externality, an industry would be in perfect competition, the producers produce to the point where the marginal revenue from sales equals the marginal private cost (as described on pages 69 to 74).

But in that case, the valuation that the last buyer places on the good is exactly equal to its price. This equality of marginal costs of production and marginal benefits to the consumers was the point that established the efficiency of perfect competition earlier. But in the case with negative externalities, we know that there is an extra cost. It must be, therefore, that the marginal value of the good, all things considered, is less than the cost of producing it.

Or, to take the road congestion case, drivers are paying the cost of fuel, depreciation of their vehicle, and a cost in terms of their own time making the journey. These are the costs they experience, and they presumably travel whenever they are less than the marginal benefit of the journey. But they are not paying for the consequence of their journey, which is the extra time that other drivers have to spend on theirs. Consideration of that means that some of their journeys have a true marginal cost greater than their benefit.

It has, for some reason, become common amongst economists to assert that these kinds of problems arise or persist because of an 'absence of property rights' or a 'lack of clarity' about them. If that were corrected, it is suggested, it would be possible for bargains to be struck which would eliminate the externality. In the case of pollution, for example, if there were a 'property right' over, say, clean air, and this were owned by the population at large, they would be able to prevent the firm polluting, or 'sell' their 'property right' to it so that it would then be allowed to pollute. The cost of acquiring the right to pollute would then become one of the costs of production for the firm and this would raise the price of the product. By this means, the consumers of the product would ultimately be paying for the full costs of production – including the cost of the pollution. If the price of the good, including the cost of the property right, were so high that the firm could not stay in business, then of course that would mean that production of the good and the consequent pollution would both cease.

In a variation of that argument, we could consider the case where the firm owns the right to the air. It would then not have to pay to pollute, but, on the other hand, those harmed by the pollution could offer to buy the rights to the air. If it were worth enough to them to reduce the pollution, they would pay enough to induce the firm to reduce (or stop) polluting. Consequently, it seems that creating the property rights, and hence the possibility of bargaining over them, would mean that the externality problem could be overcome.

That, however, is rather a limited way of looking at it. The relevant 'property right' is the right to pollute in a specified way or the right for there not to be pollution of a specified kind. If we are dealing with literal cases of pollution, then in most countries there is a mass of legislation on that kind of issue. Where there is no such legislation, that would normally mean that the polluting activity is permitted. Whenever it is permitted, the polluting firm 'owns the property right', and it is therefore perfectly open to anyone else who would like the pollution to stop or be reduced, to make an offer to that firm. In just the same way, anyone visiting a country where smoking in restaurants is permitted, and who finds themselves exposed to it, is free to make an offer to the smokers to cease. The relevant 'property right' is in that case owned by the smokers, but they can give it up if they wish. There is no need for the government to do anything to make that deal possible.

NEGOTIATING OVER POLLUTION

The idea that negotiating over the amount of pollution could theoretically always bring us to a point where the marginal costs of producing a good include the costs of pollution takes us only so far. The question of who owns the 'property right' still affects the distribution of well-being.

Consider a smoker and a non-smoker sharing a flat. In one arrangement, suppose smoking is permitted only if both agree. Here, the smoker needs to pay the non-smoker for each cigarette. On the other hand, if smoking is allowed, the non-smoker could still pay the smoker to refrain. Either way, it seems the one with the greater willingness to pay will get the outcome they want.

But consider these two extreme cases. In one, both people are rich, with one an occasional smoker who can easily go without, while the other is tolerant of smoking. In other words, neither cares very much, and both can afford to pay if they need to. In this case, it makes very little difference whether smoking is only allowed if both agree.

Now consider the opposite: there is a heavy smoker, a smoke hater, and both of them have little money. In this case the 'property right' is a very valuable, and the distribution of well-being between the two people will be greatly affected by its allocation. No doubt that case would reflect many issues about pollution and similar problems. Even if we thought bargaining solutions were viable, the fact that they achieve efficiency is not everything – there are distributional issues at stake as well.

On the contrary, the reason we do not see much in the way of such arrangements is that there are usually insuperable difficulties in bringing together all the individuals concerned, gathering the information about their preferences, conducting the negotiations, and verifying compliance with an agreement after the fact. If we label the difficulties involved 'transaction costs' – admittedly giving that term a very broad meaning – then externality and public-good problems can always be understood as arising from the presence of such transaction costs. The problem, looked at that way, is simply one of the difficulty of reaching the agreement that would achieve the social optimum.

Consider, for example, the provision of street lighting. If each individual stated the maximum they would be willing to pay for different amounts of light, then the social value of each possible amount of lighting could be calculated simply by adding the individual valuations. From this, the marginal benefits of incremental lighting could be ascertained. These figures could be compared with the marginal costs of lighting, and the point where the aggregate of the individuals' marginal valuations is equal to the marginal cost of supply could be found. The individuals would then pay the amount reflecting their valuation of this quantity and these payments would finance the lights. Just the same approach would result in the collection of payments to induce a firm to reduce pollution.

This is of course a wild fantasy at every step. Even identifying the affected individuals would be prodigiously difficult. There is a particular problem in inducing them to give an honest account of their valuations since they are in a free-rider relation to each other. Knowing that they are expected to contribute according to how much they say they value the product, and that they understand that the overall provision will be overwhelmingly determined by what other people say, each has reason to understate their valuation. There is one market failure which is the origin of the problem, then another blocking one road to its solution! It is the impossibility of dealing with this kind of thing that disables the price mechanism – not the failure to 'define property rights'.

Nevertheless, an interesting point is that in these cases, *in principle*, willing parties could make transactions that would improve the outcome. Even if that means no more than that such transactions can be imagined, it is precisely the existence of such possibilities that makes it natural to call the outcome a 'market failure'. There is scope for an improvement, but the market fails to realize it.

The natural response to such problems is perhaps to reinstate the effectiveness of the price system with a tax on the activity generating the externality (or subsidy for a positive externality). Considering the case of negative externalities, if the tax is ideally calculated then it reflects the cost of the externality. In the same way that the theoretically negotiated agreement imposes a cost on the polluter equal to the marginal damage the pollution does, so does a tax impose that cost.

Exact calculation of such amounts is not within the realm of practical policy, but some approximation can usually be attempted and there are a couple of points that emerge clearly from this line of thinking. One is that it is certainly a tax (or some similar device) rather than outright prohibition that is nearly always appropriate. For some reason, particularly in the case of serious externalities, a ban is often treated as being the natural response. But it is not. An externality is merely a cost. There are plenty of other costs in the production process, and the externality cost is not fundamentally different from the others. It is merely that the cost is not, in the ordinary course of events, reflected in the price of the good. The activity which generates the externality is activity which is achieving something worthwhile – it is creating goods valued by consumers. The problem, therefore, is to make the consumption of the good properly reflect all the costs of production.

A related point is that the effectiveness of a tax is not to be assessed by reference to whether it stops the creation of the externality. If it so happens that the tax is paid, but the generation of the externality continues almost undiminished, we can conclude that the consumers value the good enough to pay for the damage caused in creating it. So long as they do pay, the market is effective.

In a similar way, but perhaps more subtly, quantitative limits on the production of externalities miss an opportunity. We could, perhaps, aim to calculate the quantity that would be produced if we were to levy the ideal tax and set that quantity as a limit, divided up, presumably, between the producers. There are problems with deciding how to divide it, but there is another point. The real loss is this: the total quantity has been determined to be the same as would be supplied if the ideal tax were levied. The price for which that quantity can be sold is of course the same price as in the case where the tax is applied. But now the producers take all the money – none is paid in tax. The firms are prevented from supplying as much as they would like, but they nevertheless benefit from the high price. Indeed, in different circumstances they might try to operate a cartel, as described on pages 79 to 81, specifically to raise the price; but by the imposition of a quota, the government achieves that for them.

Then, the quantity of the good produced is indeed optimized, but a better solution from the point of view of public finances would be to auction the quotas – make firms pay for their limited right to pollute. They would be willing to bid the price of quotas up to the level where it is just worthwhile to buy one, and so, subject to getting the sums right, we can reach the same level of output as under the tax scheme, with the profits transferred to the public purse.

So far so good, but there are questions about the definition of externality. One would be something like 'an action which affects the well-being of individuals or the production possibilities of firms without itself being mediated through a market mechanism'. The trouble with that is that it includes pollution and congestion and all those kinds of things, and it includes people playing their music on the train, and smoking in public places, but it also includes other people wearing garish ties and loudly telling each other jokes in the pub. Some of those are easy to accept, but should people who display peculiar modern art in their front gardens be paid if others like it or taxed if they do not? Or should some people be paid and others taxed for the same thing if they live in different areas and their neighbours have different tastes?

Such interventions are unlikely to be attempted – it would be very difficult to implement such a policy even if we wanted to. The calculation of the appropriate tax would be impossible, and in some cases so would its collection. But that is not the point. The point concerns the limits of the economic theory. All those situations have a theoretical equivalence to the externality problem – the discharge of toxic waste into the river is a metaphor for them all. The theory of externalities teaches important lessons about that problem, but is entirely silent on how widely they should be applied. The reason is that there is an unavoidable ethical or moral issue about which kinds of activities should be taxed or regulated, and which are simply none of anybody else's business. Some of the issues seem easy – severe environmental damage needs to be regulated; wearing funny hats at Ascot should not be. But those are clear extremes. There are more difficult areas as well. Should those who keep dogs that bark in the night pay a tax for the disturbance of their neighbours? What about the people who organize public concerts, street fairs, and the like – they create costs in policing, noise, clearing up the rubbish, disrupting the traffic, perhaps causing congestion on public transport, and spoiling the view of the stars of some nearby amateur astronomer. Where does their liability to pay for this sort of damage stop? Is it relevant that some grumpy old residents just do not like street fairs? If it is a matter of marginal benefit, and marginal cost, where do we make the distinction between things which should be regulated, and things which should not? The answer is that the cases do all have a similarity,

which the economic theory exposes, but they are also distin-
guishable in ways about which economics has nothing to say.

Market failure and the market system

Those are only examples, but I hope it is clear that there are
varied market failures. Some of them are pervasive. We could say
that there is almost nothing that happens where each party might
not entertain doubt about the commitment of the other; a buyer
and a seller never have strictly equivalent information, and other
sorts of information problems are all around. Many of those cases
can be dismissed as trivia, although that is really a dismissal not an
answer. In many cases there is no way of telling how important
they are. If we take the idea of externalities seriously we will
find that more or less every human activity with a public aspect
generates them, and many generate the positive and the negative
kind simultaneously. Many of those may be trivial as well, but it
is an interesting problem, because it clearly shows there are limits
to what we are prepared to regard as an economic problem.
Some externalities are left alone because it would not be right to
interfere. And elements of monopoly power are likewise all over
the place – some created by regulation, some by market fixing,
some by technological inevitability, and some by the temporary
effects of entrepreneurship of one kind or another.

There is another aspect to the issue that I have hardly mentioned.
There is nothing to stop more than one market failure being present at the same time. Sometimes that might magnify the problem,
but in other cases, it can mitigate it – but make policy more difficult. If the externality-producing firm is a monopolist, it is already
producing 'too little' for that reason, even though it produces
'too much' because of the externality. Think how bad pollution
might be if OPEC had *not* raised the price of oil. But also, think

how complicated the policy problem is when there might be any number of market failures occurring simultaneously.

In principle, of course, an optimal policy response can be calculated. But that would still assume the rest of the economy is operating in perfect competition. If the firm in question appears to be producing too much, a tax will raise its price and cause it to produce less. But customers can go elsewhere – perhaps increasing the demand of a different externality-producing firm and causing *its* production to increase. Since the nature of the problem is that the externalities are unrelated to the price of the product (in the absence of a tax), it is perfectly possible that the effect would be to *increase* the production of negative externalities. In any case, the overall effect is anybody's guess. It is all very well to say that, in principle, all such problems would be addressed with the appropriate tools, and in that case we can reach an optimum. But then it is also rather important to say that in practice they will not.

So, the idea that the economist brings the tools to *resolve* these problems is a nonsense. Perhaps the economist brings the tools to understand them. But any attempt to resolve them will be very hit-and-miss.

A final point on market failure, though, is this. Considering the range of reasons to doubt that the price system works as the simplest theory suggests, it is remarkable how well it does work. It is sometimes described as a system which brings optimal results under stringent conditions. Sometimes that is put as if it makes a general and powerful case against government intervention. On the other hand, once we see how far we are from satisfying those stringent conditions, the whole proposition might seem to amount to nothing. And the fact that the 'free market' has no real existence because of government interference has little relevance to the point. Of course, government interference is commonplace. Some of it is well justified by ideas of market failure, or by other concerns, and some of it, of course, is not well justified at all. But such interference, well or badly directed, provides only a fraction of the reasons economic theory gives us to expect the price mechanism to perform poorly. And yet here we are: our morning coffee finds its way to our breakfast table. That involves an uncountable number of individual relationships with prices and profits at their heart; and it is itself only one of an uncountable number of such successes of that system. Although the economic theorist often seems obsessed with the optimizing potential of the system, that is only theory, and theory with no application. Another way of looking at it all is that the only point more striking than the huge range of market failures is how successful the market system nevertheless is.

5

Money and banks

Something that might seem peculiar about the discussion so far is that there has hardly been a mention of money. It appears as a way of measuring prices, and perhaps as something that people like to make, but apparently not as an essential component of economics at all. Part of the explanation is that – as we shall see – although money is obviously an important aspect of the functioning of modern economies, there are large parts of economic *analysis* where it is not nearly so important as might be supposed. It does nevertheless raise some issues of its own – issues concerning the nature of money itself; what makes something 'money' rather than not money; where is it that money comes from; how it is related to economic activity; and what kind of policy actions might be called for, and when?

Definition of money

Defining money is a surprisingly difficult task. The first point, though, is that in ordinary English the word 'money' is certainly used more broadly than it is in economics. As I have just said, 'money' is sometimes treated as the thing that some people like to make. But that is not an economist's usage. Really, what those people are seeking is wealth, or perhaps income. Similarly, we might say 'Mr Gatsby has a great deal of money' – but it would be unlikely to mean that his wallet was at that moment particularly full.

Confusion is taken further when economics textbooks provide a list of the functions of money. It functions, they say, as a unit of account, a medium of exchange, and as a store of value. 'Unit of account' means the measuring rod of economic value – the units in which prices are quoted. A 'medium of exchange' (or 'transactions medium') is the device commonly used to make payments, and a 'store of value' is a way of taking the power to make purchases that we have today, and moving that power to purchase into the future. But those are the *functions* of money – they are what money does. They do not exactly tell us what money *is*, or how to define 'money'.

That point perhaps comes out clearly if we consider that all the functions of money might be performed by things we would not call 'money'. The most obvious is the last of them – many things can be used as a store of value: stocks and shares, wine, land, a pile of bricks. Indeed, in principle, anything that is durable and saleable might be used to store value. Some would be better stores of value than others, of course. But that point draws attention to the fact that some of them might be better stores of value than money – in conditions of inflation, it might well make more sense to buy a house than to keep money, just to keep wealth intact.

Similarly, the unit of account could be almost anything. It would not be impossible to list prices in terms of some commodity, whilst making payments in dollars and pounds. We could, for example, imagine the case where prices were quoted in kilos of salt. So, the price of a pint of milk might be three and a half kilos of salt, or the price of a car 30,000. In that case, salt would be the unit of account, even if salt was never handed over in making a payment. In a few odd cases, something like that does actually happen – the British practice of pricing racehorses in 'guineas', each equal to £1.05, is an example. Here, guineas are the unit of account, although pounds are the medium of exchange.

And money as a medium of exchange is certainly not absolutely necessary. We know that from the fact that sometimes it is not used. Sometimes, we do swap goods for goods. It is not impossible that we might do that more often, or indeed, always.

Imagining the various situations that could exist has some interest, but little practical impact. Once we recognize that we are talking about *money*, not wealth or income, we would probably not call anything 'money' if it did not function widely as a medium of exchange. Straightforwardly, money is what we buy things with – or perhaps we should say 'what we make payments with'.

Curiously, that raises a further question: what *do* we make payments with? The answer to that will vary from society to society, and a large number of things have in fact served as a generally accepted transactions medium – sea shells and tobacco are often cited. Even the large stone rings found on the island of Yap are sometimes, rightly or wrongly, said to be money – including by the island's own tourist board. These sorts of things, though, are clearly not money in normal modern circumstances.

ORIGINS OF MONEY

A widely told story says that 'money' – perhaps in the form of precious metal – emerged of its own accord from barter exchanges. In the story, something started to be accepted by people, not because they actually wanted it, but because it was so much easier to exchange for what they did want. Once some people did that, it was even easier to exchange, and so others would be led to do the same. It is a great story about 'the free market' solving problems of exchange.

There is another view, though, which says that money emerged as a unit of account before it emerged as a medium of exchange. Values needed to be measured for such reasons as calculating compensation for injuries; and the value to be handed over as the price of a bride. With the values known, the payments might be made in any goods. That is interesting, because it makes the unit of account the historically primary function of money.

ORIGINS OF MONEY (*cont.*)

Another suggestion is that tax rules play a key role. These too require a unit of account before they require a medium of exchange. But there is a further point. An authority with the power to require payment *in coin* is in a position to mint the coins and use them to employ labour. The workers might have no intrinsic interest in obtaining the coins, but if they have to use them to pay their taxes, they have to work for them. So the government extracts 'voluntary' labour by creating the coins and the tax rules. Here, the coins can be expected to circulate widely because so many people have taxes to pay, but the existence of government is essential to the creation of money – and it is not something the 'free market' manages by itself.

A first impulse is probably to say that notes and coin – or 'currency' – are money (or 'currency appropriate to the country where the transaction is made', to be slightly more fussy). The problem with that is that many payments are not executed with notes and coin, and larger ones almost never are. The other important mechanism is the transfer of balances in bank accounts. So, for example, a person can buy something by writing a cheque, or using a debit card. The effect is that the bank debits the account of one person with the amount in question and credits that of another. Payment is thereby effected without currency – notes and coins – ever entering into the picture. Clearly something has been bought and, if we are going to say that money is what is commonly accepted in making purchases, it has been bought with money.

So, we do not go far wrong if we say that, in modern society, 'money is whatever is commonly used to make payments', and in practical terms that means 'currency plus readily transferrable bank deposits'. And again, in practical terms, money so defined will – in addition to being a medium of exchange – almost always be a unit of account. And, of course, it is unlikely that anything would be used to make payments if it were not a reasonable store of value as well – the sellers would not accept it if it were going to deteriorate immediately.

I have emphasized this as a practical rather than as an absolutely precise account of what money is, because no absolutely precise definition can be given. For one thing, if we were going to try to make it precise, we would require precise definitions of what we mean by 'buy', and what to say about transactions where neither currency nor bank deposits are used. Again, ordinary English might be a very unreliable guide. Students who buy time by promising their essay will be finished by 5:00 P.M. are not using money. There are more difficult cases than that, though. Perhaps we would say that things are 'bought' with a bribe of a bottle of whisky. It does not really make the whisky money. Some things which we surely say we can straightforwardly buy still cannot exactly be bought with money. Until recently, a ride on the New York City subway, for example, required a subway token. The token was bought with money, but it was the token that bought the ride – without the token, no amount of money would move the turnstile. The token might be called 'special purpose money' – it was a transactions medium, but only for the special purpose of buying a ride. But that is not exactly right either, since sometimes a subway token could buy something else. After all, the dollar value of the token was known to everyone in the city – there was the unit of account at work – and anyone might be willing to accept a token as a payment.

Another issue arises if we want a precise definition of 'bank deposits' (or 'bank deposits that can be used to make payments'). We would have to start by defining 'bank' – itself not an easy thing to make precise. Then there is certainly the possibility – not merely a possibility, in fact – of there being transferrable balances at institutions which are not banks. They could be very much like money as well.

All that, furthermore, is about the definition of 'money'. The economic significance of what we have just defined can be questioned too. The point about the subway tokens offers a clue – in that case, although a token was required to take a ride, anyone with money had an easy time getting a token. Well, equally, although money is required for many things, many people can obtain money very easily – by selling some other asset, probably a financial asset. So there is a whole range of assets which are 'near-money' assets in that an individual can easily sell them for money.

What those points mean, though, is merely that there is a certain amount of vagueness about what counts as money. That arises from there being a conventional aspect to money itself, and an institutional aspect to the nature of near-money. Transactions happen when there is a willing buyer and a willing seller. It is their willingness that is crucial, and there is no better definition of 'money' than that it is what is normally used in such transactions. And, in practical terms, 'currency plus bank deposits' is about as good as it gets. But then a whole range of other assets can almost be used as money as well. So, fundamental as money might seem to the modern economy, in answer to the question 'what is it?', precision is not available.

'Money is a veil'

The next question concerns what we need to say about money in trying to understand economics. One perennially popular view says: 'not much'. In this view, it eases transactions, but changes nothing fundamental. We could, as it were, imagine a magically effective barter system where the same transactions we make would occur, but without money. We could then proceed to analyse the efficiency of business, the causes of economic growth, compare the capitalist system with the communist one, or ask what determines the level of unemployment, or whatever we like, without mentioning money. In this vision, as it is sometimes put, 'money is a veil' since all it does is obscure the real economic relations.

Whether that is a satisfactory view is one that has been greatly debated, but it is beyond question that there are aspects to it which are of great importance. One is that there *are* those underlying economic relations. If we could manage a perfectly efficient barter system, we would have no need of a medium of exchange. The unit of account might still be needed, but it would be purely an accounting quantity – we might still barter a car worth $10,000 for something else worth the same amount, or pay five hundred dollars' worth of taxes, but there would be no physical tokens representing a dollar or a pound, and no bank deposits payable in those tokens. In that perfect barter system, people would still go to work for wages of known value; investors would still invest with a view to future wealth; and speculators would still speculate with the same idea. Firms would still seek to produce at minimum cost, and – in so far as they ever do – set output where marginal cost equals marginal revenue. There would still be externalities, and asymmetries of information leading to market failures, and all the rest of it. None of those things is intrinsically a characteristic of the monetary economy.

What to say about the existence of banks is slightly more difficult – mainly because it is so hard to envisage a 'perfectly effective barter system'. If it were really possible to barter labour today for goods and services in the future, then lenders might not need institutions like banks to facilitate saving. Similarly, if borrowers could obtain the services they want today in exchange for goods and services in the future, they would not need such institutions. All that, though, really does seem fanciful, although quite an entertaining subject for speculation.

A second point that the 'money is a veil' view captures is the importance of *real* rather than *nominal* values. Nominal values are those denominated in units of currency – a person's wage, in ordinary language, is a number of dollars or pounds or whatever. That is their nominal wage. If we want to know whether it is a good wage, we need to know what it can buy. The purchasing power of the wage is the measure of the real wage. (Similarly, any other magnitude conventionally expressed in units of currency would be a nominal value, and the corresponding real value would be the same thing adjusted for the purchasing power of the currency unit.) So, for example, a person's wage (their *nominal* wage) might go up by ten percent, but if the price level has gone up by ten percent, they are no better off – their *real* wage is unchanged. If the price level has gone up by fifteen percent, their real wage has gone down.

Considering the world of perfectly effective barter, the importance of real variables is immediately apparent. Whether a worker will work for a certain wage depends first and foremost on how much can be bought with that many dollars, pounds, or euros. An investor invests with a view to profit, but if it takes time for that profit to be achieved, and the price level changes in the meantime, it is the real returns that are the most important thing, not the nominal returns.

Occasionally, interesting questions come up about whether nominal variables – particularly wages – exercise any influence over behaviour distinct from the effect of real wages. It is generally noticeable, for example, that a small fall in someone's real wage due to rising prices evokes less reaction than a fall caused by a nominal wage reduction. There is, apparently, a special resistance to specifically *nominal* wage cuts. A variation on the idea is that people value their wage relative to other workers. That is certainly not to say that real wages are not important, but it does challenge the view that they are the only things that are important. The same sort of point may arise from the common reluctance to sell an asset – such as a house

– for less than was paid for it. Sometimes economists strain to explain these factors in terms of strictly rational behaviour. 'Good luck' might be the best polite response. But nevertheless, an important point is that it would be very surprising if the nominal rather than the real variables were the ones that turned out to matter over long periods of time. Workers may well resist nominal wage cuts, but if they resist them for too long, they may well find themselves out of their jobs. And, eventually, although it may take a long time, the sellers of assets must accept the market conditions.

It is sometimes said – it is quite often said, in fact – that once upon a time economic policymakers failed to understand the importance of real rather than nominal variables. This, so the story goes, was part of the explanation of the rise in inflation in the 1960s and 1970s – policymakers supposedly thought they could raise the rate of inflation, and thereby reduce unemployment. The idea was supposed to be that continuous inflation would fool workers into working for lower real wages by giving them higher nominal wages. Futhermore, it was said that it did not occur to anyone that the workers would learn to anticipate the inflation and make allowance for it in wage setting. None of that happened, of course. It is a principal theme of *Macroeconomics and the Phillips Curve Myth* to trace what did happen. But one interesting point is that anyone could imagine that the real/nominal distinction is complicated enough that such a story could be believed. It is as if economists 'forgot' the power of the point that money is a veil. As a matter of history, that is pure nonsense. The idea of money as a veil, or that it is real, not nominal, prices which determine behaviour, or the idea of 'the neutrality of money', as it is often put, is far too powerful, and far too ordinary, for any such thing to be true. It is not everything, and much of the time, it may not lead to terribly profound conclusions but it is a central idea, and has for a long time been a basic building block of analysis.

Inflation

The idea of money as a veil is certainly an important one, but it raises a question as to why there is so much concern about inflation (and occasionally its opposite – disinflation – sometimes called 'deflation'). Indeed, the theoretical case of a 'perfectly balanced inflation' would have no real effects at all. If all prices, wages, charges, fees, and benefits, as well as bank balances and the amounts of cash everyone was holding, were increased by the same proportion at the same time, and this were understood to have happened, then we would all carry on as before, with the numbers changed. An ongoing, perfectly balanced inflation would work that way as well – if all those prices and money balances crept up at a perfectly steady, known rate, and everyone understood that, there is no reason for it to matter.

MEASURING INFLATION

Properly speaking, inflation is a continuous, ongoing rise in both prices and wages (and rents and other such payments). As a *measure* of inflation we tend to use the change in average prices. That is all very well so long as such price changes bring with them compensating changes in wages and everything else, but they might not do that. If, for example, the price of oil rises, then, since oil is so important, there will be a measurable increase in average prices. That is then recorded as 'inflation' no matter whether wages change.

The problem is not straightforward because increases in important prices might lead to increases in wages, and thereby to a general inflation. But there is also the danger that what are actually simply adjustments of particular prices due to changes in supply and demand will be seen as 'inflation'. It is an important distinction because relative price changes – reflecting changes in the balance of supply and demand – are just the things we want the price mechanism to reflect. They are nothing like the symptom of 'monetary disorder' which makes inflation a problem.

Inflations are never perfectly balanced, of course. But it might be that they are often nearly so. The increase of prices is not uniform, but there is a tendency for those that begin by lagging behind, then to catch up. That, after all, is the point of the idea that money is a veil – if those prices do not catch up, money is not a veil. The currency in people's wallets does not increase – but that is a very small amount. Individuals' money held in the form of bank deposits might increase if interest rates responded quickly and precisely to inflation.

If we think of nearly balanced inflations, there would then certainly be costs, but perhaps not very large ones. One cost would arise from adjusting prices and the delays in doing so. Because of the delays, prices would be temporarily out of equilibrium, and the signals they send to consumers and producers would therefore be distorted, with a resultant misallocation of resources. Certainly there are some costs here. The costs of actually changing prices – 'menu costs', as they are sometimes called – are unlikely to be large, but in a rapid inflation, they might be frequently incurred. Or, if they are not frequently incurred, that raises the danger that some prices will be out of line with others for longer periods – distorting the signals more severely.

Beyond those, a further cost arises from the holding of currency itself. In an actual inflation, prices and payments might all move in roughly parallel fashion. But holdings of currency, since they are not adjusted in that way, continuously lose value during an inflation, and interest on bank deposits does not really keep up with the latest inflation figures. That means that, during inflation, there is an incentive to keep assets in an inflation-proof form and therefore to economize on the holding of currency (and of any bank deposits that do not pay inflation-compensating interest). We will all, as it were, carry less cash, but make more frequent trips to the ATM. Or, if no bank deposits pay interest, then we hold smaller deposits and larger sums in interest-bearing form, again with the consequential need to make more frequent conversions of these other assets into bank deposits or currency. The time, inconvenience, and expense of making these transactions, or trips to the ATM, are therefore a cost of inflation – sometimes called 'shoe-leather costs'.

Still, these costs of inflation at low rates seem small. One reason is that it has been assumed that everybody knows inflation is in progress. In fact, not only are inflations never perfectly balanced, they are never altogether predictable either. Nor is the problem just one of predictability – there is also a question as to whether inflation is correctly perceived immediately after it has occurred or while it is occurring. Both the extent and the duration of the misalignment of prices that might occur when inflation is volatile and unpredictable are almost bound to be much larger than the costs associated with slow inflation.

In practical terms we should probably add the point that the general confusion that can result adds further difficulties. It might be, for example, that some individuals or groups are able to take advantage of the situation by achieving higher wages for themselves. The benefit to them may be temporary, but the disarray they cause is still a cost to everyone else. One way of looking at the issues of misperception and general confusion is that precisely what they do is impair the operation of the price mechanism. Rethinking the section in chapter 1 about the price mechanism, it is apparent that what was being assumed – 'implicitly assumed', since it was not stated at the time – was that economic agents were aware not just of the money-prices they face, but of the relative prices that were relevant to their decisions, including those in the near future. One of the problems, perhaps the biggest problem with realistic, somewhat unbalanced inflation, is that it makes it hard to discern what are the relative prices that do or shortly will prevail. That scrambles the messages of the price mechanism, impairing its operation, perhaps seriously.

Some of these issues also raise the possibility of inflation having something of an automatic tendency to accelerate. If, for example, inflation is so fast that the buying of assets to protect against it is sufficiently extensive, then that process itself might affect a wider and wider range of goods. The first move to purchase assets tends to raise their price; the second move then might focus on other assets. Further inflation then results from the attempts of individuals to protect themselves against the inflation that already exists. It also could be that, for example, feelings of unfairness that arise when prices are temporarily distorted eventually give rise to more and more aggressive wage demands, or calls for political action to favour certain groups. These things too might have a tendency to speed inflation. And, of course, at high enough rates of inflation, the shoe-leather and menu costs themselves become substantial. In the worst cases – cases of hyperinflation – the shoe-leather costs can be so great as to bring a complete collapse of the monetary system.

There can also be benefits of inflation. For example, sometimes, state payments, tax reliefs, or other things of that kind are recognized as being too high, but it is politically difficult to change them. Just as a matter of practicality, it may be easier to allow them to be eroded by inflation.

A variation on that would concern workers employed in a declining industry. It might be that the conditions of demand for the product are such that, if they are to keep their jobs, their wages need to fall. Since inducing workers to accept a nominal wage cut often proves very difficult, a gentle inflation, combined with stable nominal wages, may – again, just as a practical matter – keep them in jobs better than anything else. Since it has the effect of easing adjustment in the labour market, this is sometimes called the 'lubricating' effect of inflation, and whilst the theorist who insists on strictly rational behaviour will struggle with it, that alone is not sufficient reason to reject the idea.

Inflation, banks, and the supply of money

On the basis that *high* rates of inflation, at least, are a problem, the next questions must be about what causes it and what can be done to prevent it. One very common presumption is that inflation is caused by there being too rapid a growth in the quantity of money, and, therefore, the solution is to reduce the rate of growth of the quantity of money or, as it is sometimes informally put, for the government to 'print less money'.

That view can certainly be made to seem plausible. The 'money is a veil' thought suggests that real variables are determined independently of the monetary system. 'Money', however, is used in making transactions, but it then seems that 'money' is more or less just another good which happens to be used in nearly all transactions. Then it seems perfectly natural to say that, if there is a larger quantity of it, other things being equal, each unit will have lower value. And, finally, the government (or central bank) is responsible for issuing currency, so it must be that the decisions about issuance ultimately determine the value of each unit of currency.

To my mind, that is an example of an economic model which, despite its antiquity and perennial popularity, is useless or worse in handling the problem to which it is addressed. Indeed it is a beached whale of a theory: massive, ancient, imperious, and – because entirely unsuited to the context in which it finds itself – very dangerous. Monetary systems simple enough for the theory to have some relevance once existed but, in the modern world, it describes nothing of any insight.

First, money is not merely a transactions medium. Consequently, the quantity of money that individuals wish to hold varies. If, for whatever reason, individuals wish to hold larger money balances than previously, then, even on the theory just suggested, an equivalent increase in the total supply of money does not affect prices. If they wish to hold smaller balances, a constant supply of money cannot guarantee price stability.

Perhaps more importantly, most money is not 'printed' by anyone; and indeed most money is not created by the central bank or the government. Mostly, it is created by banks in response to the wishes of their customers. For that reason, increases in the quantity of it are at least in large part the consequence of decisions of economic agents and result from their (more or less) rational, optimizing behaviour. Growth in the money supply, if that occurs, is at least as likely to be the effect of other economic developments, including inflation, as it is the initiating cause of inflation.

This indeed is a reason why it is so important to recognize that bank deposits – or some bank deposits – are a form of money. It is important because the next point is that bank deposits can be, and often are, created by banks by means of making loans to their customers. This strikes many people as surprising since it is easy to imagine that bank balances are created when individuals go to a bank and deposit currency – they leave a bag of money in the safekeeping of the bank. Then, it seems, the bank might take some of that and lend it to someone else, and it might then be redeposited by that or another person and, in due course, re-lent. That could happen, but in the modern world it is unusual. In the first place, individuals walking into banks with currency to deposit is not the most common way of adding to a bank balance. Much more common is a transfer – a salary payment, for example – from someone else's bank account. But, more importantly, when a bank makes a loan, it does not do it by handing over a bundle of notes to a borrower. It does it by crediting that borrower's account. The loan takes the form of the electronic equivalent of writing down some numbers in a book.

When that loan is made, a deposit is 'created' in the sense that the borrower's balance is larger than it was. But the money then in that account has not been printed, and indeed it has not 'come from' anywhere – the bank does not wait for someone to make a deposit before writing that number in a book; nor does it deduct anything from anyone else's account when it makes a loan to a customer. Consequently, the conclusion is inescapable that the making of that loan has increased the total of bank balances. The bank has created money.

This can be a hard point to understand. One way of looking at it is that in making the loan the bank simultaneously creates an asset and a liability for itself. The asset is the loan – the bank is owed money by someone else. The liability is the deposit – that is money the bank must transfer to someone else's bank account on the instructions of the borrower, or hand over in the form of cash to the borrower. The seemingly odd thing about it is that since payments can so easily be made with bank deposits, the liability it has created for itself is 'money' in the sense that it is a medium of exchange. So, another way of looking at it is that, from the point of view of a bank's customers, whether their deposit at the bank has arisen through them taking money and depositing it, through someone else transferring a deposit to them, or through the bank crediting them with a loan amount, it makes no difference to the fact that they can spend that deposit. The balance in their account is money they can spend – however that balance arose.

All this arises because it is a distinctive characteristic of an economy with a reasonably sophisticated banking system that the liabilities of the banks are accepted in payment. Because of their ability to create liabilities, such systems are quite different from more primitive ones – including the primitive ones suggested by some economic models where the 'quantity of money' is controlled by the government operating a 'printing press', or the number of sea shells that happen to be available, or whatever it may be.

It could well be said, of course, that there are factors limiting how much money a bank can create. There might be a legal limit of some kind. But beyond that, there must also be a prudential limit. A bank that creates too many deposits – that is, makes too many loans – creates the danger that many of these customers will withdraw the deposits. Most likely they would make payments to the customers of other banks. In that case the first bank needs to be able to make a payment to that other bank. It might do that in a variety of ways. It could send over a truck full of currency – but then it has to have the currency available; or it could write a cheque drawn on an account it has at a third bank – such as the central bank, but then it has to have a sufficient deposit at that bank. Here, though, what it cannot do is 'print money' to pay: when a bank creates deposits, it is creating deposits for its customers. It cannot create money and credit it to itself.

That puts a limit on how much money a single bank can create. But, if all banks are expanding their balance sheets in this manner at the same time, each will not only be losing deposits to other banks, but taking them from other banks as well. So, when the whole banking system is making loans and thereby creating deposits, it might be that none of the banks individually finds itself consistently making transfers to the others. That removes a significant constraint on the creation of money by the banking system.

In terms of understanding inflation, there is a further point. The quantity of money might respond to the price level. Consider this possibility – the creditworthiness of a business customer depends in large part on their profit or turnover. But if there is inflation, then prices rise, and unless other things change, the profit and certainly turnover of every firm rises. That is, they rise in *nominal*, not real terms. But, despite that, every firm thereby becomes worthy of a larger bank loan – again in nominal terms. Indeed, if money is a veil, it will need a larger loan in nominal terms when the price level is higher. So, in an entirely rational world, inflation can bring changes in the quantity of money. Consequently, the mere fact that the price level and the quantity of money tend in general terms to increase in a similar way, shows nothing about the causes of inflation.

A response to all this might be to say that banks could be subject to such regulation as to bring their money-creating under the control of the policymaker. It would be interesting to see whether the attempt to regulate them to that extent would result in the creation of more bank-like institutions which could provide similar loans. Indeed, in an extreme case, it could even lead to the creation of money-substitutes in the form, for example, of corporate promises to pay. If so, the regulatory problem could become enormous. Whether the restriction of bank lending in this kind of way would even be desirable is another question. Both the ability of banks to make loans and the possibility of making payments by transferring bank deposits are, as things stand, essentials of our economic society. The idea that we should regulate banks to prevent them from creating money, or to allow them to do it only on terms strictly determined by the central bank, does rather create the impression of trying to redesign the world to make it fit an economic model. We surely should be careful about that.

None of this, it might be said, is to doubt the view that if there were a sudden increase in the quantity of money for other reasons, that could cause inflation. The arrival of huge quantities of South American silver in Europe in the sixteenth and seventeenth centuries led to inflation. If a government did simply run a printing press to produce more paper money, very possibly that would have the same effect. Producing large quantities of forgeries of an enemy's currency has been contemplated as a weapon of war on the basis that, if dropped on cities, it might create enough inflation to destroy their economy. The point, though, is that this is not the only way inflation might come about.

Controlling inflation

So, the next question must be, what *does* it take to control inflation? If we understand 'inflation' as being merely an increase in average prices, then anything which increases some prices without reducing others causes inflation. On that basis, commodity and food price increases, energy bills going up, and similar events are causes of inflation. (And when such prices fall, there is disinflation.) That, though, is not a very satisfactory way of thinking about the meaning of 'inflation'. The *problem* of inflation is one of an ongoing, general increase in both prices and wages (and other payments). There have been some very heated debates about what causes that but it may be helpful to distinguish two polar views.

In the first, inflation is the result of widespread excess demand – that is, demand being greater than supply across a wide range of products. In that situation, output might rise, but unless we are starting from a position of unemployment and excess capacity, that will not go far. The reason is that, if the excess demand is general, particular firms will find it hard to employ more resources without paying more for them, and if they do that, costs rise, so we can expect prices to rise. Demand might be too high for any number of reasons – government expenditure increased, raising demand for goods and services by the government; taxes were cut too much, raising demand by the private sector; there was an export boom; house prices rose so much that people started to feel much richer than before, and so spent more; or optimism about future prospects developed, again leading to more consumer expenditure. Here, there can be an aspect of the process which is self-sustaining – the high level of demand raises not only prices, but also incomes, and thereby creates the spending power for a yet higher level of demand. And this is, of course, just the kind of situation that would lead to an increase in the quantity of money through the making of more and larger loans. Consequently, there may be no quick and easy way in which such inflation burns itself out.

Another possible explanation of inflation is that prices increase because of a rise in the costs of production – such as wages, fuel costs, or whatever it may be. But in this case the rise in costs is the initiating factor, not itself the result of excess demand. When costs do rise, of course, prices rise and, again, it might be that such an inflation has a self-sustaining aspect in that, with higher nominal incomes, costs can again be raised. Aggressive trade unions seeking wage increases which in fact brought inflation, and then making a bid for further wage increases, is often thought to be one aspect of the inflation of the 1970s.

Needless to say the theoretical distinction between 'types' of inflation need not match reality at all – different causes can be mixed in the same period of inflation. So, for example, the build-up of expenditure on the Vietnam War in the second half of the 1960s probably started American price rises – that was excess demand. But the rise in the price of oil in 1973 added a cost aspect. And the acceleration of inflation itself may have fuelled union demands – even beyond compensating for the price increase.

In seeking to control inflation, the natural response is to meet excess demand inflation by reducing demand. That might be achieved by raising taxes or interest rates. If inflation is caused by cost increases, then preventing those increases would control it. Some cost increases probably cannot be prevented. In the case of wage increases there is at least a temptation to think that they might be controlled by some sort of agreement. In the 1960s and 1970s numerous such 'incomes policies' were tried in many countries. The idea was that such things as presidential urging, or nationwide agreements between unions and the government, would result in lower wage increases and thereby reduce inflation.

It was never an easy matter to rationalize that idea in terms of strictly rational behaviour by those involved. The answer to that might be that wage bargaining is not a strictly rational matter, of course. But in any case, in the 1970s it very much seemed that such policies did not work. Either the presidential or other urgings went unheeded, or the agreements were not made, or having been made, they were not kept. So, in the end, such direct methods were abandoned.

All that remained was to control inflation by reducing demand. At this time, the idea that the best way of controlling demand was specifically by controlling the quantity of money became briefly fashionable. That put monetary policy, and central banks, at the forefront of inflation control. The high interest rates that followed reduced inflation, but also raised unemployment. The fact that unemployment rose is suggestive that the inflation was not simply a matter of excess demand. That might mean that there were aspects of cost inflation. But, by that point, inflation perhaps had an aspect of 'momentum' so that wages and prices were raised because of a general appreciation of the inflationary environment, rather than because of any specific cost or demand consideration. To what extent, in the end, it was the reduction of demand that controlled inflation, or the reduction of demand that brought unemployment, and the unemployment which put a stop to aggressive trade unionism, is something that is very hard to determine. But, certainly, it was when policymakers focused on the reduction of inflation, and allowed unemployment to rise, that inflation was brought under control.

What followed was interesting because policy attitudes generally were transformed. During the 1980s and 1990s it became very widely accepted that, in terms of the control of inflation or unemployment, variations in government expenditure and taxation were much less effective than monetary policy, and the main concern should therefore be to keep government borrowing as low as possible; and meanwhile monetary policy should be controlled by 'independent' central banks and that they should focus continuously, and perhaps exclusively, on achieving inflation rates in a very narrow band – such as between zero and two percent. Indeed, enthusiasm for these ideas was one of the considerations promoting the creation of the European Monetary Union since, it was felt, with the independent European Central Bank to control inflation, and other rules controlling government borrowing, effective economic policy was assured. It was not to be – but that is a matter to which I shall return.

6
Growth and unemployment

In this last chapter I am going to consider several matters concerning economic prosperity. One of those concerns national income and its growth – why it is that economic prosperity generally rises as time goes on. The second is the question of unemployment. That was considered in chapter 2, but, as I said then, there was more to be said about it than that the equality of the marginal product of labour with the wage might ensure there was no involuntary unemployment. Third, the relationship of monetary and fiscal policy as tools available to the government. And, finally, the financial crisis. That topic does, as it happens, bring together many of the lines of argument of the preceding pages.

National income

The 'productive potential' of an economy might be described as the full-employment national income. It is the 'full-employment' income because we assume for current purposes that all productive resources are employed – that is what gives sense to productive *potential*, rather than actual production. The idea of 'national income' is that it is the total of the value of all economic product in a country. A difficult issue arises over what is meant by 'economic' product. The answer – unsatisfactory though it is – is that it is the final product that is sold. Here, 'final' means that we are interested in the value of the product which is sold to its final users. Without that qualification we would end up adding up the value of raw materials sold to one firm, to the value of its output which is sold to another firm, and adding that to the value of the product of the producer of the final goods, and adding again to the price at which it is sold to the consumer. At each stage, the price includes the value arising from the earlier stages of production. That is not what we are interested in – it is only the value of the goods as they emerge from the whole chain of production that we want.

Determining what is a 'final' good might result in some ambiguity, but I said the definition is 'unsatisfactory' because by focusing on what is sold, it makes the calculation crucially dependent on what happens to be marketed rather than, for example, produced within a household. So, in a society where domestic services are undertaken by family members, there is work being done, but it is unmarketed and not included in national income. In a society where those services are paid for, national income is higher, even though it may be that just the same things are being done, but they are done for payment, rather than within the household.

One thing about the definition which is important is that it does include *all* marketed goods and services. There is, for example, no discount for what some might regard as frivolous products. Golfers earn their salaries by entertaining golf-watchers. The market valuation of that entertainment is what it is, and from those market valuations we can find out the contribution of the players to national income. Meanwhile, the market valuation of bakers is what it is, as is that of soldiers, politicians, and academics. No ethical judgement, or judgement of moral worth, is incorporated so as to weigh these contributions to national income. Conceptually, the same is true of illegal activities producing marketed goods and services, and legal activities conducted in a clandestine way to avoid tax. They may not appear in the official statistics, but that just means the statistics are wrong.

The natural and obvious way of addressing the question of why some countries have vastly greater productive potential than others is to consider the quantity of productive resources they have. 'Productive resources' would certainly include such things as labour and capital, including communications infrastructure, but also natural resources in the form of oil, precious metals, and useful rare elements, but it would also include things such as the amount and fertility of agricultural land and fish supplies, as well as anything else with economic value – including, for example, value in attracting tourists. The pyramids at Giza are not exactly natural resources, but, like the Grand Canyon, they generate income for the inhabitants of the country where they are located.

That, however, does not take us very far. For one thing, skilled labour is very different from unskilled labour – and there are many different sorts of skills as well. And, perhaps even more than in the case of 'money', the exact definition of 'capital' is elusive. It certainly includes equipment and machinery which enhances human productive capability. But it might be said that the skills of labour are best thought of as a kind of 'capital' as well. That is an interesting economist's metaphor: 'human capital' is the knowledge and skill of a person which enhances their productivity 'just like' machinery.

An important aspect of capital, which provides one basis of its distinction from land, is that it usually takes investment – involving a sacrifice of consumption or leisure – to acquire it. If it is cabbages we are trying to grow, we may well grow more when we have a tractor, but to build the tractor there must be labour which is for a time working, but not on the cabbage field. It is this characteristic which suggests counting learned skills as 'capital'. Students – those in college and MBAs alike – while they are studying, are unproductive. Instead of studying, they could be working and producing something, or enjoying leisure. So, in either case, capital is acquired by investment, and investment requires a sacrifice of current consumption or leisure.

Capital, technology, and growth

That reasoning makes it natural enough to see the accumulation of capital as the route to national prosperity. Natural resources are more or less given and the quantity of labour depends most of all on the number of people. But the amount of capital – including human capital – a country has depends on its history of investment. So, allowing for natural resource endowments, rich countries will be those that have accumulated a large amount of capital.

Now, in considering the accumulation of capital, an important issue arises concerning the marginal productivity of capital. That is the question of what happens to output as the quantity of capital increases, with the quantity of land and labour being held constant? This question reflects the consideration of marginal effects in various other chapters, and following the pattern of argument there, the natural assumption is that the marginal product of capital falls – as a country acquires more and more capital, the increment to output attributable to the marginal unit declines.

If that is so, then the returns to investment, in the form of increased output, decline and very probably become zero. At that point, further investment gets us nowhere. A slightly stronger point along the same lines would be that capital needs to be maintained. If the marginal product of capital is low enough, then the extra output arising from the last unit of capital will be less than required to maintain that capital. We would then be better off, in terms of output available for consumption, with less capital.

That is a powerful insight because it suggests that more and more investment might cease to raise income. It says it is possible to reach a point of capital saturation. That does not quite dismiss the importance of investment since with a growing population it is still necessary to acquire more capital – it is the ratio of capital to population that is the crucial consideration. And, of course, the fact that there exists a point of capital saturation does not mean we have arrived at it. Indeed, some countries obviously have not. There, investment remains crucial.

Nevertheless, under the assumed conditions, capital accumulation will eventually cease to yield any benefit. As it stands, that is quite an interesting idea. It suggests that the process of capital accumulation is one that goes on only in a phase of history. At the end of it, we reach a point where there is no benefit in further capital accumulation, or, if we look at it that way, where capital has ceased to be scarce. There ceases to be a proper *economic* problem about capital.

That does, however, suggest the question of whether there is anything else to be considered, and most economic analysis has taken the route of considering 'the level of technology' as distinct from 'the quantity of capital'. The idea of the level of technology is that where technology (including design, management technique, and so on) is more advanced, more output can be extracted from the same quantity of land, labour, and capital. It is as if $10,000 dollars' worth of capital at a 1945 level of technology is less productive than $10,000 dollars' worth of capital at a 2015 level of technology (having allowed for changes in the price of capital). Looking at it that way suggests that continuing economic progress depends on advancing technology, in addition to accumulating capital.

But that also raises a familiar question – what happens to the benefits resulting from technological progress as the level of technology rises? Or, to put that in more familiar terms: what are the marginal returns to technological improvement? We have, for the time being, assumed that the marginal product of capital declines. Is the same thing true of technological progress? Might there even be a point of technological stagnation as well, where 'improving technology' yields nothing in the way of economic benefit?

Now those are very problematic questions. The metaphor we are invited to consider is that of the addition of extra labour or extra capital to a productive process. There, it seems natural to suppose that the increment to output of an extra person or an extra machine will eventually fall. We are invited to consider whether the same is true of an extra step in technological progress. But the question is, what is a 'step' in technological progress for which an 'extra worker' or 'extra machine' is a useful metaphor?

We might, pursuing that issue, decide to call the invention of polyurethane a 'step'. Then the question is what else, coming later, is a 'step' of the same size in the advance of technology? Only when we know that could we consider the question of whether later 'steps' produce less marginal economic benefit than earlier ones. But the question plainly has no answer – there is no way to define these steps. As far as pursuing the idea of diminishing marginal product is concerned, we have reached the limits of the metaphor.

MEASURING 'CAPITAL' AND 'TECHNOLOGY'

The idea of the 'marginal product' of a factor of production raises the question of how to measure the quantity of a factor of production. We have to do that so we can consider the question of how productive is 'one more unit' of the factor. Considering the case of capital, we cannot do it by something like counting machines, because not all machines are the same. There is a temptation to do it by measuring the value of capital. But then there would be the issue of whether we mean 'cost of production', or 'market value

MEASURING 'CAPITAL' AND 'TECHNOLOGY' (*cont.*)

at a point in time'. The first will not do because it would suggest economic theory says that if only we spend enough money on building capital, we can raise national income. But if we measure the quantity of capital by its market value, then we have to face the point that the market value of a machine depends on the market value of what it can produce. But it does not seem right to say that the *quantity* of capital in a car factory changes because the price of cars goes up or down.

Measuring 'technology' raises the same sort of problems, but in a starker form. If we wanted to test an idea such as that the marginal benefit of technological advance declines, we would want to identify 'equivalently sized' technological advances. So, for example, starting in the United States of 1900, by what year had there been as much technological advance as there was between 2000 and 2015? If we knew that the answer to that was, say, 1930 – so that technology advanced as much between 1900 and 1930 as it did between 2000 and 2015 – we could then start to compare the *economic benefits* of these equally sized advances of technology. But how do we measure technology so as to be able to do that?

There is another way of looking at all this, however. That starts by questioning the value of the distinction between 'capital' and 'technology' but emphasizes the point that the usefulness of any piece of capital equipment, which of course embodies a particular technology, itself depends on the level of economic development.

To illustrate that idea, we might consider this caricature. If we have to hammer in one nail a year, we can probably manage by using a stone. If we have to hammer in many nails, it might be better to start by making a hammer. Making the hammer is an investment – some capital is acquired by the sacrifice of leisure or the making of consumption goods (or the hammering of nails with a stone).

Making a hammer to hammer one nail a year would be absurd – it would take too long for the investment to pay off. But at a higher level of development, where economic output is higher, there are more nails needing to be hammered. It may well be that, at that higher level of development, 'technology' has advanced and the making of a hammer is also easier, but the interesting thing here is that it is not essential to the argument that it should be so. Merely the fact that there is more hammering to be done makes the investment worthwhile.

That thought can go further. If there are enough nails to be hammered, we would be best off starting by making a hammer-making machine, and using that quickly to produce many hammers. And at yet a higher level of development, we might want a machine to make the machines that make the hammers.

That is, as I say, a caricature. Call it an economic model if you like, and if you do, I hope it is the best illustration yet of how a model which is factually absurd can guide thinking towards insight. A more general way of putting the point would be that there are an infinity of ways of getting a particular job done. They can be ordered according to how roundabout the process is. We can hammer nails with a stone; we can stop to make a hammer, and then hammer the nails; we can stop to make a hammer-making machine and then make the hammer, and then hammer the nails; we can make a machine of higher order to make the first machine, and then the hammer, and so on. At each stage, it would take us longer actually to hammer the first nail. But if we have enough nails to hammer, the quickest way to getting them all hammered could be to take a more roundabout route.

The same kind of reasoning will be applicable to any piece of equipment. And, of course, it will be true that there might not actually be 'machines that make the machines that make hammers'. Rather, there are machines designed with flexibility to make many different things. But that adds another layer of reinforcement to the line of thinking. What makes it worthwhile to invest in the design and construction of a flexible machine-making machine is that the general level of development is such that it pays to make all kinds of different machines.

There are two ways in which that picture is quite different from the one based on 'capital', as a factor of which there might be a particular quantity, and 'technology' as something else determining how productive that capital is. First, there is no clear distinction between 'more capital' and 'better technology'. Capital accumulation and technological development are not quite the same process, but they are processes which naturally occur together. The hammer-making machine is not exactly 'better' or 'more technological' capital than the hammer. At some point in the process of economic development, that machine is produced, but that need not exactly be because at that time someone *invented* it; it could just be that it is only at a certain stage of economic development that there would be any point in making it. So it does not exactly represent technological progress, in the sense of the fruits of research. On the other hand, it is not exactly just 'more capital' either, because in a primitive society it would be simply useless – it would not be capital at all.

The second point is that this way of thinking invites us to see the process of economic growth as self-propelling and cumulative. It is not straightforwardly that 'investment' occurs, thereby raising productive potential. It is the increase in economic activity which makes the investment worthwhile. And it is not that technology is at some point discovered, thereby giving new powers to existing factors of production. Rather, it is that investment takes different forms at different stages of economic development. It is the economic development that creates the need for sufficient hammers that makes investment in the hammer-making machine a viable proposition. But the investments – in hammers, and hammer-making machines – certainly do increase productive potential, and thereby set the scene for further increases in output and further rounds of investment, perhaps in developing yet more roundabout means of production. With capital and technology both seen in this way – intrinsically linked to expanding production – it is perhaps easier to envisage a process without diminishing returns to investment, and so to see economic progress free of eventual stagnation.

We might add a couple of further thoughts. One is that it might be that the cumulative process of investment in more and more roundabout means of production has more scope in some activities than others. It might be, for example, that in the production of manufactured products there are more possibilities than in agriculture or services. And, bearing in mind the cumulative aspects of economic progress that this view suggests, it could be that countries which *first* start to produce manufactured products are able to keep on advancing the way in which they are produced – thereby raising productivity per person more and more. Whereas, those which initially lag tend not to reach the point where domestic production of manufactured goods reaches sufficient scale for the most advanced techniques to be viable. Once lagging behind, in other words, the inducements are to import efficiently produced goods manufactured elsewhere whilst remaining substantially agricultural themselves. If that is the case, then relative paths of economic development can be 'history-dependent' in that those off to the quickest start have a long-term advantage. That is obviously important in its own right, but it is notable that it also offers a second commentary on the idea of comparative advantage considered in chapter 1. In the text box there I suggested a reason to doubt whether the idea of comparative advantage makes as powerful a case for free trade as it seems. That argument was based on how changes in demand might leave some countries worse off. The argument here – pointing to the same sort of worry – is one about the development of supply. It may not be immediately apparent how distinct they are, but in fact they approach the issue in quite different ways.

Either way, though, we see one of the limits of the metaphor of comparative advantage. If the countries producing some goods are put on a superior development path to others, that difference may eventually be much more important than the immediate gains from exploiting current comparative advantages. So, it could be in the long-term interests of a country to ignore the benefits of trade and seek the superior path of development. It is an unfortunate conclusion because all countries might well face the same incentive. Instead of the cooperation promoted by the price mechanism, we might face trade protectionism designed to develop the industries with the progressive potential.

None of this means that it is wrong to think about why different countries have different productive potential in terms of the quantity of productive resources they have. But it does put the question of the acquisition of productive resources into a different light. For one thing, there is a suggestion that the idea of the possibility of 'stagnation' may arise from the wrong way of looking at the process of economic growth. And for another, it might be that some of the most important issues concern how the process of growth gets underway in the first place, or how it can be given a sufficiently powerful impetus in countries which lag behind.

Another kind of observation entirely is this. I have now suggested three different ways of considering innovation and technological advance. In chapter 3, innovation was what a particular firm might do in order to get ahead of its rivals. That could be something that depends on advanced research, but it could, as I said, be purely a matter of display. In this chapter, it was first about a general sense of the level of technological development, with that level being understood as something that determines how much could be produced with a given quantity of capital, land, and labour. And third, it was a matter of the kind of capital that is useful at different stages of economic development. What are we to make of there being three different ideas about it? There is no question of one of these being 'right' and two of them 'wrong', or even, really, one being better than the others. There are three ways of thinking about the issue, each of which brings some enlightenment, and none of which, properly speaking, has a claim to providing, or even pointing in the direction of, a 'science of the economics of innovation'.

Unemployment

The discussion of productive potential is certainly an important aspect of economics, but it is not to be forgotten that the issue of whether actual production reaches the level of potential is another. One reason it might not is that the productive resources are used inefficiently. Any of the market failures considered in chapter 4 can have the effect of limiting production to less than potential. In addition, there are such things as union restrictive practices, bad management, and the government employing people in pointless activities – or even in those which are actually damaging to other people's productive activities. Another reason, though, is that productive resources might not be employed at all – there might be unemployment, not just of labour, but of any factor of production.

In chapter 2, I promised further consideration of that issue. In that chapter, thinking about how many workers a single firm wished to hire, it was reasonable to think of its decisions as affecting no one but itself, and its own workers and customers. Such firms were treated as optimizing against a background where nothing else was changing – 'other things were equal'. A different view arises from thinking of the 'labour market' as a whole and 'the goods market' as a whole, and considering the relations between them. The difference is that when we think of the problem in these terms – we think of it macroeconomic-ally – we have to consider the point that, if *all* firms are trying to hire more labour, sell more output, reduce the wage they pay, or whatever it might be, these things affect the economy as a whole and it ceases to be appropriate to suppose 'other things are equal'.

In this case, the crucial point is that there is demand for labour (or any factor) only to the extent that there is demand for the goods and services that it can produce. This leads to the possibil-ity that an insufficiency of 'aggregate demand' – meaning the total value of demand for all final products – might be a cause of unemployment. The point is that if there is no buyer, there is no seller, and if there is no seller, there is no job.

The buyers might be people – or 'households' as for some reason economists always say. They also might be firms, but while we are concerned with final products, the relevant purchases by firms include, for example, new capital equipment, audit, and externally provided staff training. Their purchases of raw materials, and of semi-finished products, are not purchases of final products. Governments make purchases of goods and services, too – battleships, services of tax inspection, street clean-ing. And it is to be remembered that purchasers can also be in a different country, making for 'exports' – although the purchasers themselves are foreign households, firms, and governments. But without some buyer – including, perhaps, buyers who are wast-ing their money, or creating employment out of a philanthropic motive – there is no seller.

In exploring some implications of this, the starting point is to appreciate the equivalence – the strict identity, in fact – of 'income', 'expenditure', and 'output' (all three considered in aggregate terms and in terms of money values – so it is 'the total value of all individuals' income', etc.).

I shall begin by treating households, taken as a group, as being the owner of firms, and supplying them with labour; as having income determined by their wages and other payments from firms, such as dividends; and consuming final products sold by firms. That could naturally be interpreted to mean that *some* households own the firms whilst others provide labour to them, and so on. The point, though, is that the households as a group are the ultimate owners of all the productive resources. Then there are firms which, in addition to hiring factors of production, including labour, owned by the households, also purchase new capital equipment in the form of, for example, machinery. Firms – again treating them as a group – are also the producers of those capital goods, as well as the consumption goods purchased by households.

I shall assume, for the time being, that there is no international trade, no government, and wages and prices never change. As usual, the question 'Is it true that prices never change?' is no more interesting than asking, 'Is it true there is no government?' We can assess the model when we know where it leads.

Here is where it leads. The total purchases of final goods are the total of firms' investment – their expenditure on new capital – and households' consumption expenditure. The total of receipts by firms for their sales of final product is the same thing – the amount spent by the buyers is the amount taken by sellers. So the value of expenditure equals the value of output.

The income of households is again the same thing, so long as we understand by 'income' the total addition to their wealth from all sources (not the money actually paid over to them which, for example, would be counted as income by the tax authorities). So, households obviously earn wages and dividends. The sum of those is not necessarily the same as the proceeds earned by firms from their sales since, for one thing, there might be retained profits. But that is one of the ways in which the point that the households (collectively) own the firms is important. Any profits retained by the firms are, since they are held by the firms, owned by the households. In that sense they are part of households' 'income'.

It is possible to become confused by the fact that firms supply services and intermediate products to other firms, so some of the proceeds from the sale of final products go to these other firms. Indeed they do, but these other firms are owned by households, as are any other firms, further down the chain, which supply them. Similarly, natural resources that are used in the productive process are owned by households (or by firms which are owned by the households) so that payments for them also accrue to the households. The point is that each dollar paid for a final product ends up in the ownership of the households – it might be paid to them in wages, it might be paid in dividends, it might be paid to another firm, but from there it ends up as wages, or dividends, or it might be retained profit, but then it is owned by the households. There is, as it were, nowhere else for that dollar to 'go'. And consequently the 'income', in this extended sense, of households is also equal to expenditure, and to the value of output. Income equals expenditure equals the value of output. This is the first point.

Now, expenditure is made up of households' expenditure on consumption goods and firms' expenditure on new capital goods. On the other hand, the only thing households spend income on is the purchase of consumption goods. The rest of their income is not consumed – it is 'saved'. So, looking at where households' income comes from, it is total expenditure: consumption plus investment. Looking at how households use their income, it is equal to consumption plus saving. That has the interesting consequence that the saving of households has the same value as investment by firms.

That might seem to be a long-winded way of stating the obvious – saving and investment are in a way two sides of the same coin. But it is a subtler point than it seems. For one thing, the idea that, as is sometimes said, including by undergraduate textbooks, that households save by making bank deposits, and these deposits are then borrowed by firms for investment, has nothing to do with the point. That line of thinking, even if correct, is an irrelevance to the point being made. Banks are simply not part of the story. In the argument I presented, we reached the conclusion that saving equals investment without even mentioning the issue of how investment is financed, or anything like that. The conclusion arose from thinking about the relationships between expenditures, receipts, firms, and households.

Indeed, I can go rather further than that and say that nothing about agents' *behaviour* has been assumed at all. The point that households' income equals consumption plus saving is much more like a fact than it is like the outcome of an analysis of what households, acting rationally or irrationally, might do. It is just that there are only two things that can happen to their income, so when we add up the income going to those two uses, we have the total of income. The same can be said of the point that the sources of income are consumption expenditures and investment expenditures. Consequently, there is a good case for saying that what we have so far is not really a 'model' at all. Rather than being a model, it is more like a list of definitions, with some observations about how they fit together.

A natural response to that is perhaps to say that the definitions are very restrictive – as are the assumptions about, for example, there being no international trade. However, once the pattern of the argument has been appreciated, it is easily broadened in a multitude of ways. Here is one example. Suppose we allow households to spend income on investment goods. In this case, firms' proceeds are the sum of households' expenditure on consumption and investment goods, and firms' expenditure on investment goods. So that is also the income of households. In this case, households can do three things with their income: spend on consumption goods, spend on investment goods, or save. We are back at the same point: saving by households has the same value as investment by firms.

Here is another: suppose we introduce the government and say that it levies taxes on households and makes expenditures. Again, firms make three kinds of sales: consumption goods to households, investment goods to firms, and government purchases. And households have three uses of income: consumption, saving, and paying tax. So, we could say 'consumption plus investment plus government expenditure equals consumption plus saving plus tax'. That leads not to 'investment equals saving' but to 'investment plus government expenditure equals saving plus tax'. (If we make the further assumption that government expenditure equals tax revenue, then of course we are back to saving equals investment – but government expenditure does not always equal tax revenue.)

We could introduce imports and exports, making the matter yet more complicated. Here we have to be careful to remember that, for example, 'consumption' means 'consumption of domestically produced goods'. But we end up with saving, plus taxation, plus expenditure on imports equals the sum of investment, government expenditure, and the value of exports.

Alternatively, we could vary the categories of agents by, for example, having 'firms', 'households which own firms' and 'households which do not own firms'. Then, in the simple initial case, we end up with investment equalling the sum of saving by the two types of household. And extending the question to the various other cases results in longer and longer lists of things to add up, but no fundamental change. There is no fundamental change because, deep down, the whole story is little more than an elaboration of the point that for every sale there is a purchase, and for every purchase a sale. There are any number of variations in the way we could categorize buyers, sellers, the kinds of things they buy and sell, and transfers, such as tax payments, between them, but they are only a matter of categorizing things, not really a matter of explaining them at all.

Well, if it is just a matter of categorizing things, someone might well say, 'So what?' One important consequence is this. If there is to be a change in the total value of any of household saving, firms' investment, government expenditure, tax revenues, imports or exports, then there must be corresponding changes in some or all of the other quantities.

So, for example, we might consider the case where, starting from a position of full employment, households collectively decide to save a greater proportion of their income. There is a temptation to say that the result is that since (in the simple case, without the government) saving equals investment, investment must rise. But that is much too quick a move. It is a case of allowing the most obvious piece of mathematics to determine what the economic behaviour must be. Here is another possibility. When households decide to save a greater proportion of their income, what they do is consume less. There is, after all, not exactly any 'action' of saving – there is only refraining from spending. But if households collectively consume less, firms sell less, and households collectively receive less income. If nothing else changes, the fall in household income is exactly the same as their reduction in consumption. In that case, the value of their saving has remained *unchanged*. There is then no problem explaining how it comes to be equal to investment – they are both the same as they were (although the households' desire to save a greater proportion of their income has been fulfilled – by their income falling).

Each of those views – either investment rises or income falls by the same amount that consumption fell – are very simple ideas. But they produce starkly different results – we either have an investment boom or a recession. In taking the matter further, we are in the realm of modelling, properly speaking. We must consider the behaviour of agents in a situation where households as a group are seeking to save more.

One idea might be that the additions to saving will have a

tendency to lower interest rates and thereby promote investment. One difficulty is that additional saving might not take the
form of placing funds in financial markets. It might be just that
money is put in a sock. That is saving, but it surely does not
lower interest rates. Another would take us into the realm of
questioning what determines interest rates and whether there
is anything that makes the increase in investment reliably equal
the fall in consumption. For one thing, that would seem to
depend on the availability of viable investment projects, which
can hardly be guaranteed. There is another kind of difficulty
that is apparent on thinking a little more deeply. If investment
is going to rise because the extra saving has reduced interest
rates, then it is necessary that there actually be extra saving. But
what has been described is a fall in consumption. In so far as
that brings a fall in income, there is no unspent income that is
saved. Even more than that, we might feel that circumstances
of falling consumption are not naturally those in which the
acquisition of new capital would seem the best strategy to most
firms. Indeed, those circumstances are those where it might
appear rational to invest less, thereby promoting a further fall
in income. Still, assumptions are assumptions. If we *assume* that
the fall in consumption is met with an increase in investment,
then we reach the conclusion that an attempt to increase saving
both succeeds and brings extra investment.

If we consider the same problem with taxation and government expenditure in the picture, there are more possible variations, but no fundamental difference. When households consume
less, the value of firms' sales of consumption goods falls. Taken
alone, these things mean that income falls. The fall in income
may very well result in a reduction of tax revenue and an increase
in government expenditure. The reduction in tax leaves households with more post-tax income than they would otherwise
have had, and allows some increase in saving; the increase in
government expenditure is itself a source of sales for firms and

mitigates the fall in income arising from the fall in consumption. Still, we must reach a point where saving plus tax revenue is the same as investment plus government expenditure. In this case, saving does increase, but – if investment remains unchanged – only to the extent that government expenditure has increased and tax revenue fallen.

In practical terms, a 'fall in income' is, of course, the same as a rise in unemployment. If income has fallen, the value of output has fallen. On the assumption that prices stay the same, the quantity of output has fallen, so someone is out of a job. A straightforward way of looking at it is that the people previously employed in producing the consumption goods that are no longer bought have become unemployed. With that thought, it is immediately intuitive that those people, now unemployed and with no income (or severely reduced income), will be saving less than they were, and therefore that other households can be saving more. But the aggregate of saving is equal to the aggregate of firms' investment. So, those who remain employed may manage to increase their saving – but the total of saving is equal to investment. Except in the case where changes in tax and government expenditure wholly offset the fall in consumption, income must fall (unless investment rises).

We could start the story at a different point. Suppose we start from a situation in which there is widespread unemployment, and firms decide to increase investment. They therefore decide to place orders for capital equipment (or staff training, or whatever). The fulfilling of those orders results in increased employment for the producers of that equipment or providers of training and hence increased output and income. No doubt there will be extra taxes paid, and perhaps a reduction in government expenditure. And, since there are people now employed who were previously unemployed, it is natural to suppose that aggregate saving will increase. The outcome must be that, one way or another, the increase in investment minus the change in government expenditure (if any) is exactly balanced by the increased saving plus the increase in tax revenue.

We could equally start with the government. A government which, for example, wishes to reduce its deficit might try to do so by raising taxes and reducing government expenditure. But, as with the attempt by households to save more, the excess of government expenditure over taxation can decrease only if the excess of private saving over investment decreases. The policy might have that effect − for example, because those making investment decisions are impressed by the government's policy. Or, on the other hand, it might have the opposite effect − by reducing sales to households (which are paying more tax) and the government itself, the policy might lead households to fear their own unemployment and so seek to increase saving. In that dismal case, the government's attempt to reduce its deficit is actually self-defeating: it makes it worse. But whatever the reactions of the private sector, the crucial point here − a desperately poorly understood but crucial point − is that the government deficit is not simply a number that the government can choose. Nor is it a number it can choose if only it is 'determined' enough. It is a number affected by the government's decisions, but also in part an outcome from the operation of the whole economic system.

I have not said much about changes in imports and exports. One collection of additional possibilities is that a change in saving or investment, or whatever, will be balanced by changes in international trade. So, for example, a fall in consumption might be met by an increase in exports. In the extreme case where the increase in exports is equal to the fall in consumption, unemployment is unchanged. In that case, there is the further question of what is happening in the other country − one country exporting more must mean another is importing more. If those imports substitute for domestic production, its employment has fallen, or if for imports from elsewhere, then someone else's exports have fallen. In the world as a whole, the problem is not solved, although for one country it might be. Unless someone, somewhere, is buying more, there cannot be a general increase in selling.

All these ideas result from recognizing that the behaviour of large groups of agents – 'households collectively', for example, or single large agents, such as the government – cannot be analysed on the basis of 'other things remaining equal'. When we are thinking about a single individual (or individual firm, or small group of people or firms, and so on), the problem is a different one. A single household that wishes to save more can reduce consumption and thereby save more. It must be true that someone sells less because that household is consuming less, and whoever that is (or someone from whom they reduce purchases) will save less as their income falls. But that does not make it impossible for the first household to save more, nor to analyse its behaviour on the approximately correct assumption that it affects no one else.

But to suppose that we can consider one such agent and treat it as representative of all of its kind, and hence that approximately correct analysis applying to one is reasonable analysis applying to the group, can be a serious mistake. It involves what is sometimes called 'the fallacy of composition' – the mistake of supposing that aggregate behaviour reflects that of the 'representative agent'.

It should be clear that one serious issue raised here is about the determination of unemployment. The analysis of chapter 2 is all very well for a representative firm (or worker), but it ignores the point that in the aggregate, thinking about each firm's optimization of its production cannot be enough if we say nothing about the determination of aggregate demand for the products of firms collectively. On the other hand, the analysis of chapter 2 did emphasize the effects of wage changes on firms' hiring, and in this section, I assumed wages never change. No doubt, a natural thought is that if, for example, a fall in consumption leads to a fall in output and hence unemployment, wages will fall, and somehow that will sort out the problem. Clearly then, the significance of the fixed-wage assumption must be considered.

Certainly, a single firm, observing that it can hire workers for a lower wage than previously, will, other things being equal, hire more. But to suppose that is enough is plainly a fallacy of composition. And thinking further suggests the problem is much more complicated. A *general* reduction in wages immediately and directly reduces the income of wage-earning households. We have to consider the further consequences of that.

The first point to consider is the effect on prices. Since wages have fallen, costs have fallen, so we might suppose that competitive pressures would drive down prices. To the extent that this happens, it means *real* wages have not fallen. If we suppose other factor prices also fall in line with wages, then firms have no reason to hire extra workers. For each firm, the quantity of output at which marginal cost and marginal revenue are equal is unchanged. So employment is unchanged.

We can make the opposite assumption. Suppose prices do not fall at all. In that case the profit margin on each sale is increased. The households which receive those profits will therefore have an increased real income if the level of output stays the same (or rises). On the other hand, the real income of households which receive wages but not profits certainly declines. So the profit-receiving households will consume a greater quantity of output while the wage-earning ones consume less. On that basis, there might, overall, be greater or lesser sales.

A slightly different way of looking at the same issue is this. If, following the wage reduction, extra workers (or extra factors of production generally) are employed, they produce extra output of a certain value. The households collectively (including the newly employed ones) will receive that value as income. But if they save *any* of that extra income (and nothing else changes), the increase in purchases will be less than the increase in output. That means that some of the extra goods will have to go unsold.

In this case, those extra workers will either not be employed, or will not stay employed. That much is true whatever happens to wages.

Something else might change, of course. An attractive possibility is that the reduction in wages brings an increase in investment. Then unemployment can fall. It is an oddity of the situation that the fall in wages, since it may not in itself increase output, may provide no reason for extra investment. And increased investment would have reduced unemployment even without the reduction in wages. So, the decision to increase investment looks as if it is not quite rational. But still, if it is the reduction in wages that leads to the investment, the result is a fall in unemployment. And, one might say, there is a kind of self-fulfilling rationality about it.

Another clear possibility is that falling wages, which bring some reduction in price, might improve a country's international competitiveness, and thereby increase exports. As already noted, that reduces unemployment in one country, but in itself does nothing to raise aggregate demand in the world as a whole, and cannot reduce world unemployment – we might say the fall in wages has resulted in the 'export of unemployment'.

So, we have in this argument an important story about the relationship of the so-called 'macroeconomic aggregates' – consumption, investment, saving, and so on – and some particular consequences for the analysis of government deficits and unemployment, as well as an illustration of the trouble that can be caused by thinking in terms of 'representative agents' as a way of analysing economy-wide phenomena.

But we also have an example of a seemingly crucial assumption – that there is no change in wages or prices – but which is, in fact, of much less significance than that. Rather, the thought that, if only wages would fall, any problem of unemployment must be resolved is more of a distraction than anything. It distracts attention from appreciating the importance and implications of the point that there are no sales without purchases. Certainly the question of what actually happens to wages and prices will be part of the whole story. It is not to be *believed* that they are unchanging. But the *assumption* that they are is a useful step in discovering the key relationships.

Monetary and fiscal policy

Once we reject the view that all it takes to achieve full employment quickly is the flexibility of wages, it becomes apparent that any *automatic* forces tending to bring unemployment to an acceptable level may be very weak. When, for example, a recession begins, it might be a long wait for investment to rise, or households to decide to reduce their saving. Conditions of recession are not naturally regarded as a time to refrain from saving, or to initiate business expansion. So, the question arises as to whether a government's 'macroeconomic policy' can be useful. Usually the options are seen to be to act through either fiscal policy or monetary policy, with exchange rate policy perhaps being another possibility.

Although attitudes were different in the early postwar period, monetary policy tends to be thought of as the primary tool of macroeconomic policy. That concerns either or both the quantity of money and the rate of interest. Although there have been different views at different times, most policymakers think in terms of the central bank's control over interest rates as its primary tool. The impression is sometimes given of the central bank actually determining interest rates. As the newspapers say, they take decisions to 'set interest rates'. Actually, of course, the rate of interest on any particular loan is a matter for the borrower and the lender to agree – and there is a very wide range of interest rates actually prevailing at any particular time. Generally speaking it is simply no business of the central bank what they agree.

There are, however, mechanisms by which they can influence interest rates. One is that they can determine rates of interest in their dealings with commercial banks. In practical terms, banks usually need to have deposits at the central bank, and the interest paid on those can be determined by the central bank. The central bank has similar power when banks find themselves borrowing from it. Either of those might influence the interest rates at which commercial banks deal with their customers. That influence might be mechanical in that the banks set their rates on the basis of the central bank's rates, although there is little necessity for them to do so. So it is sometimes suggested that the central bank's influence might arise as much from giving a lead to the market and settling expectations on particular numbers rather than through any compelling, market-driven effect.

Another possibility is that the central bank might become a buyer or seller of government bonds (or private sector bonds, although that is rarely done). By buying such bonds through 'open market operations', it would raise their price and thereby lower the interest rate, and at the same time increase the amount of money held by the sellers of those bonds. This would be an 'easing' of monetary policy in that interest rates were lowered. If the interest rate on government bonds were reduced, then they would become less attractive and so to some extent there would be more demand for other bonds, and hence they would have higher prices and lower interest rates. In this way, open market operations can, if conducted on a sufficient scale, affect interest rates generally, although there would clearly be some uncertainty about the extent of the effect.

A further issue then arises as to what effect the change in interest rates has on economic activity. Sometimes there seems to be a simple presumption that lower interest rates make for more borrowing and hence more investment and consumer spending. Lower interest rates might reduce the incentive to lend, of course, which would then have the opposite effect. They

certainly reduce the income of those with interest-earning financial assets (whilst reducing the expenses of those for whom they
are liabilities). But in any case, the magnitude of any effect is in
question. We might think of the question of taking a loan to
make long-term investments in building or expanding a business. It is difficult to believe that small differences in interest
rates make much difference to the desirability of undertaking
the investment, considering the very large uncertainties that will
in any case exist. A more powerful effect might arise through
such things as the change in interest rates being associated with
a change (in the opposite direction) in asset values, and hence in
the value of collateral that a borrower can offer. In that case the
effect of, say, lowering interest rates would be to raise the value
of collateral and, rather than having much effect on the desire to
borrow, thereby make it *possible*. If that is how it works, though,
it is particularly clear that the magnitude of the impact of interest rate changes on investment spending would be both hard to
measure, and uncertain.

That still leaves the case where the interest rates closely affected
by the central bank are so low that there is no practical scope for
lowering them further. This creates a motive for 'quantitative
easing'. In this case, central banks purchase financial assets – in
the same sort of way as expansionary open market operations –
but the point is to leave the sellers, which are mainly banks, with
larger quantities of money, rather than to lower interest rates.
In the particular context of the global financial crisis of 2007–8
and its aftermath, that had the benefit of putting the banks' ability to meet their immediate obligations beyond doubt. But the
further hope is that the availability of this extra money will lead
to more lending by the banks. It is 'quantitative' easing because,
to the economist, what stands in opposition to 'quantity' is not
'quality', but 'price'. Since monetary policy cannot be 'eased' by
lowering the price of loans – the interest rate – it is made easier
by changing the quantity of money. Again, though, the effect

on economic activity is questionable because it depends on the availability of creditworthy customers to whom the banks might lend, and more than anything, that depends on the availability of good investment projects.

A different mechanism, but sometimes an important one, operates through the exchange rate. If, as is often the case, interest rate reductions (or quantitative easing) reduce the foreign exchange value of a currency, then this has the effect of making exports cheaper from the point of view of foreigners. Thus, the fall in the exchange rate can lead to a fall in unemployment. Meanwhile, imports are more expensive – that may create some employment as well, since domestic producers competing with imports are in a stronger competitive position. On the other hand, it also has some effect in raising the price level.

It is difficult to place much reliance on effects operating through the exchange rate because they are hard to control – the power of international financial markets is so great. Also, unwanted exchange rate changes can impede effective policy. That was one consideration leading to the creation of the euro – it removes the possibility of exchange rate changes between the member states. That, though, has also removed the possibility of a seriously recession-hit country benefiting from a fall in its exchange rate.

In the context of macroeconomics, 'fiscal policy' is policy over the aggregate of government expenditure and taxation. Obviously there are important issues about how the government spends money, and which particular taxes it chooses to levy. They, however, are not at the fore. Rather, we are considering choices about the aggregate values of these two things. In particular, following the line of thinking of the previous section, the crucial consideration is the size of the government deficit (or possibly of its surplus) – the difference between tax revenue and expenditure. That is readily and conventionally measured as a percentage of national income so, for example, a 'three-percent

government deficit' means that the excess of government spending over tax revenue is three percent of national income. As
we saw, the government cannot actually determine that, since
the outcomes of its decisions are linked to the outcomes of the
private sector's decisions. Nevertheless, it can form an intelli-
gent appreciation of the effect of their actions and set plans and
targets on the basis of those. And certainly it can take specific
actions to change government expenditure by, for example,
undertaking or stopping specific infrastructure projects, and
changing the number or payment of civil servants. In the case
of tax, normally it would change the rules – by, for example,
changing tax rates or bands. When it does that, the change in
revenue that results will be uncertain, since it depends on how
the change in the tax and the change in the size of the government deficit (or surplus) affect the number of people employed
and how much they are paid.

An advantage of fiscal over monetary policy is that it can
be made to affect employment more directly. The example of
undertaking an infrastructure project is clear-cut. If the government does that in conditions where the appropriate factors of
production are unemployed, jobs are immediately created. That
is part of the significance of 'government expenditure' being one
of the components of aggregate demand. If the employed people
were previously unemployed, it would be surprising if they did
not also consume more when they are given that job; and that
is a further increase in aggregate demand. The opposite occurs
when expenditure is reduced. Similarly, changes in personal tax
rates have an immediate effect on the post-tax income of households. Their effect on spending is then less certain, but it is easy
to see that there is likely to be some.

On the other hand, for demand to be expanded by such
things as undertaking specific expenditures, we would want
there to be planning of those expenditures and that makes it hard
to change policy quickly. The idea that unemployment can be

reduced at a moment's notice by employing people to dig holes and fill them in again is correct as a piece of economics – the diggers and fillers do have jobs, and national income is increased to the extent of government expenditure paying them, their own expenditures, and any other expenditures resulting from their having jobs. But it would be much better to employ them doing something useful.

A further issue concerning fiscal policy is that of the sustainability of government debt. When government expenditure exceeds its tax revenue (and any other sources of revenue it has), there is a government deficit. For the most part that is financed by borrowing. Government borrowing is nearly always borrowing from the private sector (not from other governments) and, very often, substantially from the private sector in the government's own country. It takes effect by the government selling a bond to a private agent (very possibly a bank). When particular bonds come due for payment, it is quite normal for another bond to be sold to repay the first. When, as is often the case, governments undertake additional borrowing year after year, the total stock of government debt rises.

The (almost) ever-rising stock of debt is not a problem for a government in the way it is for a household since, in normal times, there is also economic growth, and hence a growth of the tax base. This means that the government's ability to service its debt is also increasing. For this reason, the overall indebtedness of a government is usually measured by its debt as a proportion of national income. There is, of course, some limit to a government's ability to repay (or even service) its debt by means of tax revenue. But the mere fact of the debt continuously growing does not mean that limit will ever be exceeded. The idea that it is *essential* eventually to balance the budget is – so long as there is growth of nominal national income – complete nonsense.

Indeed, we can go further. One step is to say that it is not absolutely necessary for the government to finance expenditure by a combination of taxation and borrowing at all. It is possible to finance some of it by the creation of money. The central bank can credit the government's account – in the same way that commercial banks credit a customer's account when they make a loan – and the government can make payments from that account. The government has then 'borrowed from the central bank'. But if the central bank is regarded as an element of the government, that amounts to nothing, and in any case, there is, as regards the economics rather than any legal provisions, no compulsion on the central bank to require repayment. Here we do have an electronic version of 'printing money' – government expenditure is financed by the creation of new money. But so long as payments in the form of that money are accepted by the private sector – as they surely are in all but the most exceptional circumstances – it is a way of financing government expenditure. For that reason, the debt ratio in itself cannot constrain the spending of a country which has its own currency. It could equally be said that the existing debt could be repaid by 'printing money'. One consequence of this is clearly to obscure the distinction between 'monetary policy' and 'fiscal policy', since there can be such a thing as a 'money-financed fiscal expansion'.

That exposes one of the problems of the European single currency. The governments or central banks of the EU member states do not have the power to create euros. Only the European Central Bank can do that. So, those governments can only finance expenditure (including interest and debt repayments) through taxation, borrowing, and various sorts of hand-out from the ECB and other international organizations.

It may well be argued that a large financing of government expenditure (or repayment of debt) by the creation of money in the way described would cause inflation. In many circumstances it surely would – it is not to be presumed that the creation of money offers the government a free lunch. The point, though, is that 'government borrowing' is not like the borrowing of a household, for two reasons. As discussed on pages 144 to 157, the government is so large that its expenditure and taxation decisions have macroeconomic effects, and those should be kept in mind when its decisions are taken. Secondly, though, it does have more options in financing repayments – including, perhaps, those that might lead to some inflation. Particularly in times of crisis, that should be clearly appreciated, if for no other reason than that all possible responses to a crisis can be properly considered.

The crisis

And so, what of the crisis? After a serious problem of inflation in the 1970s, most of the world economy seemed to settle down to much more stable conditions from about the mid-1980s or slightly later. This came to be called 'the Great Moderation' – and it was subsequently suggested that the business cycle had been cured. It seemed that central bank independence, inflation targeting, and fiscal discipline had brought economic stability. Whether ongoing low inflation resulted from these things or it happened that they were adopted just as inflationary cost pressures were disappearing is hard to say. But it is fairly clear that a belief in the effectiveness of the new way of making policy bred rather more complacency than was realized at the time. It was a period of low inflation but, as we now know, that was not enough to ensure continuing economic stability.

As the story is usually told, the problem at the root of the crash was excessive and irresponsible mortgage lending in the United States. When the American property market turned down in 2006, many of the assets based on these mortgages became worthless. The failure of Lehman Brothers in 2008 spread panic, and in particular led to the failure of AIG. Meanwhile, the uncertainty and panic that spread in financial markets around the world contributed to the bursting of the property market bubbles in Ireland and Spain. In the former, the necessity of bailing out the banks led the Irish government to a position where international action was required; in Spain, the collapse of the construction industry led to a recession, and for that reason serious fiscal difficulties. There were some gigantic bailouts of financial institutions, and the realization that the government of Greece was in no position to pay its debt led to further international bailouts.

That is all very well, and there are many books and other sources with much more detailed accounts of events than this. But recounting the sequence of events, and even identifying the specific mistakes that were made, stops a long way short of explaining how such a disaster could occur – how was it that so many bad decisions were made, by people – private agents, regulators, central banks, and governments – who were supposedly experts, that the world economy was put in such a vulnerable position? And all that having happened, why has it proven so hard to return to a world of steady stable growth of the kind that was made to seem normal in the 'Great Moderation'?

One recurring theme in accounts of how all this happened is that of moral hazard. Those involved in irresponsible sub-prime lending were surely not acting in the true interests of their employers. That is an interesting case because many of them were apparently earning large bonuses designed to incentivize them. On the face of it, those bonus schemes are a response to a moral hazard problem – without the bonuses, the workers make insufficient effort. The theory must be that without those bonuses, they would have made too few loans. But with them, they made a great deal of effort of the wrong sort. To call the schemes badly designed is certainly not an overstatement, and it is almost possible to form the impression that the idea of 'moral hazard', perhaps not very well understood, was more of an excuse for huge bonuses than it was their rationale, is it not?

There are probably aspects of moral hazard, as well, in the failure of so many regulators to prevent irresponsible lending. In some cases their failure was so spectacular that it really might call into question whether there is any point in having such regulators. But, in any case, there is a very strong impression that they lacked the necessary incentives to adopt a tough line when that was what was required. Perhaps they were subject to a degree of 'regulatory capture' whereby the regulator finds life much easier if they give their subjects plenty of freedom.

The moral hazard aspects of the problem can be overplayed, however. There are other things to consider. One concerns the question of whether bankers were led into irresponsible lending by the fact that others appeared to be making money out of it. If so, behaviour which was in fact foolish could easily be seen to be justified on the basis that since so many others were doing it, and since they were such highly paid, and presumptively skilful financial analysts, it must really be a good idea. That must have been mixed with wishful thinking, and no doubt also with the fear of being the only one to miss out on the bonanza. They are just the sorts of reactions that it is easy to imagine are important in financial markets generally, but which the efficient markets hypothesis seems to make impossible. We should now all learn the obvious implication about that hypothesis. But there is also more than the suspicion that the prevalence of that hypothesis itself deterred serious enquiry into the sustainability of asset values. The government of Greece, for example, was continuing to borrow – that is to say, financial experts, controlling other people's money, were continuing to lend to it – long after it should have been apparent that Greece could not repay what it had already borrowed. It is hard to explain that outcome without the prevalence of the idea that 'the market' is so efficient that the fact that the lending still continues proves that the borrower is sound. (The fact that some of the official data was wrong comes nowhere near providing a sufficient explanation.)

One aspect of the banking crisis which seemed to have come as something of a surprise was the fact that there could be a 'short-term creditor' run on a bank. I described the problem of depositor runs on pages 95 to 96. But some banks borrow by issuing bonds rather than, or as well as, by taking deposits. Those bonds can be short term and, when they are due, need to be repaid by renewing the borrowing – by selling another bond. As soon as there are serious doubts about the reliability of ultimate repayment, the selling of those new bonds can in effect become impossible. The effect is just like that of a depositor run in that the bank is unable to meet its immediate obligations – and the situation has the potential to have just the same mixture of rational and non-rational behaviour. But these creditors are not covered by deposit insurance, so that does nothing to prevent the run. It is something like that which accounts for the failure of Northern Rock in the UK.

A further point concerns the externality aspects of bank failures and near-failures. A run on one bank can make others appear unsafe. But so interlinked is so much of the financial sector, that the actual failure of one institution can bring about the failure of others – that was exemplified by the aftermath of the failure of Lehman. In either of those cases, there is a negative externality which is part of the story – the risk-taking by one institution not only puts itself at risk, but puts others at risk, as well. The knock-on consequences of the failure of Lehman have also raised the question of whether such institutions should be treated as 'too big to fail' – in other words as being so important to the financial system that they must not be allowed to fail. If so, that really would raise a moral hazard since no one would have to think twice before lending to an institution like that, and so, presumably, it would borrow at very low interest rates. So the externality and moral hazard issues become intertwined.

There is a different externality when a bank either fails or comes near enough to failing to be forced to reduce its loans.

Then its borrowing customers need to find another bank. When it is only one bank that is in difficulty, that may present no particular problem – so there is an externality there, but a negligible one. But when a large number of banks are troubled at the same time, then there can be a general contraction of lending, and that has an adverse impact on non-bank firms which might otherwise have been perfectly sound. One consequence of that is that some businesses which had every expectation of being able to repay their loans may not be able to at short notice and hence there is a further turn of the screw. Consequently, the kind of crisis management which is appropriate to a single failing institution is not appropriate to the kind of general collapse which threatened in 2007–8 – forcing a large number of banks to reduce their loans simultaneously makes the overall situation worse. There is another fallacy of composition in thinking that an appropriate remedy when one bank is in trouble is equally appropriate when many are.

Ideas of moral hazard have been very much to the fore, too, in arguments about responding to the crisis – particularly in the case of over-indebted governments, and most particularly in the case of Greece. It is technically a simple matter to cancel the Greek debt. The European Central Bank is the issuer of currency. It can create as much money as is required, buy the Greek (or any other) debt, and then announce that repayment is not required.

The issue of whether, in this case, that plan should be resisted as likely to cause inflation clearly needs to be considered. It is difficult to see how that can be a serious objection. Bailouts of the Greek government have the effect of creating money, so that has already been done, and if it is inflationary, the die is cast. In any case, the quantitative easing policy is designed precisely to increase the money supply. So it can hardly be a point against debt cancellation that it too would have that effect. And despite these things, policymakers have in fact become worried about falling prices, so that if anything, an impetus to making them rise would be helpful.

A different story is that bailouts of governments create a moral hazard because they set a precedent – other governments would be induced to borrow too much, spend it, and then similarly appeal for a cancellation of their debt. Such a policy would lift any constraint on government spending. A government could spend as much as it chose, finance it with borrowing, and then ask for a bailout. If the bailout is forthcoming, there is no need ever to impose taxes and then lenders, anticipating the bailout, have no reason to doubt that they will be repaid. That is probably also a recipe for hyperinflation: since government expenditure would be unconstrained, it is very likely that it, plus private sector consumption and investment, would make for excess demand.

So we end up in a position where bailouts are limited and conditional on severe policy restraint. The doctrine at work is that we must have twenty-odd percent unemployment in over-indebted countries because they must be punished. If they are to have a bailout, they must pay, and must pay in a currency that will deter others from overborrowing.

An equivalently over-indebted household would certainly declare bankruptcy and be done with it. In the case of a euro-zone member country, that would probably require the reintro-duction of a national currency. That is because sufficient of the assets of a country's banks are usually in the form of government debt that, if that debt became valueless, the banks would also be insolvent. They could be allowed to fail, in which case the country would lose not only its savings and loans institutions, but also much of its payments system – there would be no bank accounts against which cheques could be written. So, a govern-ment would wish to rescue the banks, but it could only do that by recapitalizing them with new money – and in the euro, the government cannot produce that money. Leaving the euro would be traumatic, perhaps, but on the other hand, the government's finances would be instantly transformed by its being released from its debt obligations.

Whether, in any case, the moral hazard problem applying to government borrowing is properly treated in this way is another matter. The punishment that is applied to a 'country' is actually a punishment applied to its people. By a giant stretch of the imagination, they, or the older ones amongst them, can be seen as responsible for what happened since they elected the government which got into debt, or allowed it to happen. But realistically, the burden falls on people who are far removed from the decision-making process that led to the problem. Not only is it absurd to think that justified, but since it punishes people who were not the real decision makers, it is far from clear that it addresses the moral hazard issue in any case.

More than that, though, the austerity programmes seem to pay next to no regard to the fiscal arithmetic discussed on page 153. Monetary policy clearly has not rescued the eurozone from the consequences of the crisis, although even quantitative easing has been embarked on only with some reluctance. But in so far as any attention is paid to fiscal policy, it seems only to be concerned with balancing the budget, or coming as close as possible to that, or perhaps even to actually seeking a surplus – even in countries where there is no difficulty about borrowing more. So far are we from considering monetary financing of debt that recessions are worsened by the attempts to reduce government deficits. Although the results were much worse than official forecasts, they were easy to foresee: if government expenditure is to be cut, there is either going to be less expenditure all told, or some other sort of expenditure will have to rise. Neither private consumption nor investment is likely to rise much in the circumstances. Exports would be a possibility, but demand in the rest of Europe, at least, has not been so buoyant as to raise imports to the level that would be required. Worse than that, the

European response to the crisis has been such that the euro area as a whole has been exporting more than it has been importing, with the result that world demand is retarded.

I certainly cannot give a full account of the crisis, its origins, or policy responses – apart from anything else, there are simply too many aspects to it. But it is interesting that there are so many points at which readily understandable pieces of economic analysis have relevance to it. Moral hazard problems – or something enough like them to be mistaken for moral hazard problems – are all over the place; externality problems make some appearances; and the efficient markets hypothesis – or its deficiencies – looms in the background. The basic fiscal arithmetic seems to have been pushed out of policymakers' minds, despite the insight it offers. Furthermore, in none of these cases is it true that the points were never appreciated. It is much more as if there was a lack of appreciation of the variety of ways in which some of these ideas might *matter*. It is almost as if the mathematical exactitude with which they are presented in the academic literature, by valuing that kind of scientific precision, distracts attention from the matter of bringing into consideration breadth of thinking, or an appreciation of the range of insights the models might offer. Or perhaps it is not 'almost as if' that is the case. Perhaps that is precisely the case.

7

Conclusion: a science for the citizen

Economics is in danger of getting a bad name. There has for long been mockery – sometimes derision – over the apparent artificiality of 'models', and sometimes over the fierce disagreements between economists. The artificiality of the models, I have tried to show, should not in itself be a detriment. As to the reputation for dispute, to a large extent, those disagreements have often been presented as having faded away, to be replaced by the orthodoxy which – so it was supposed – created the 'Great Moderation'. But the hubris over that is a greater condemnation than all the discord that there used to be. And in answering the Queen's question – 'Why did no one see it coming?' – it should definitely not be enough to point to one or two who did. Why did *everyone* not see it coming? Nor is that by any means the extent of it – it should not be forgotten that the euro did not happen by accident, and nor is it a natural phenomenon. It was *designed* to be the way it is; designed with all the power and insight provided by the best – or what was supposed to be the best – of the economics of the 1980s and 1990s. Yet it proved to be a catastrophe.

There are more weaknesses in economics than that. One persistent failing is the tendency of theorists to snatch at an argument that works in logic and follow the line of rational thinking, and then presume it correct, or to limit the range of candidate theories with strict criteria of rational behaviour and select between them. As I hope I have shown, there is plenty of insight in the study of rational behaviour. But a critical appreciation of its limits is an essential in assessing the models. Far too often, economists are so caught up in the game that they do not realize it is not actually real life.

And then there is the mathematics. Without question, most economists will consider a piece of research serious only if it is presented mathematically. Indeed, it is impossible to specialize in economics, even in undergraduate studies at a good university, without much of the work being mathematical. And consequently a priesthood is created. Seemingly, only those possessed of these mathematical skills can be 'economists' and everyone else must await the fruits of their expertise. Some might suggest that economists, since they lack the government-sponsored, cartel-creation rules of professional licensure, have found a different way to create barriers to the entry of their profession. Certainly, as with those licensed piano teachers, there are unlikely to be frequent complaints from those who benefit, in prestige or otherwise, from the existence of this priesthood – 'An *economist*, educated at Oxford and Harvard!'

Something that is certainly an outcome of this is that this leads to the promotion of people whose interests are primarily in the mathematical aspects of the problems. Another is that, having invested so much in the mathematics, it is not easy – just as a matter of ordinary psychology – then to take seriously the problem of describing the *limits* of the work. Yet, as I hope has become clear, for economics to be consistently useful, an appreciation of the limits of the models is essential.

Anyway, it is definitely not the case that mathematical skills are required to participate in the discussion. On that, the priesthood should simply not be allowed to have its way. Despite appearances, and despite the benefits to economists of making their professional skills seem essential to participation, economics can be a science for the citizen. It certainly should be that, as well, as it plainly affects us all. But there is more than that, because the euro and the crisis show that economists have failed, and failed dismally. The idea of the 'Great Moderation' was, as much as anything, that it was a celebration of the triumph of economics. The failure of the 1970s had been overcome and, just as importantly, the discord of the 1970s had been overcome, as well – there was a new consensus; macroeconomics had been understood. *No it had not*. Economics can and should be a science for the citizen; and economics must be a science for the citizen, because we need to get it done better than it has been.

But reacting to the crisis is by no means the whole story. Economic discussions, or economic prejudices, or opinions about people or their work derived from observations about economics are so much a part of the fabric of contemporary discussion that economic judgements are all but unavoidable. Those are by no means the things that are emphasized in economics textbooks, but one way or another, they do shape and form very much of so many people's vision of their world. And those matters, or a great many of them, are intrinsically matters of debate. They should be debated, and shame on the economist who, ever again, hides behind some pretend consensus of the economists' priesthood to say that expertise has triumphed, and no one else is really part of the conversation.

Notes on sources

The idea that economics describes the 'logic of life' comes from Harford, *The Logic of life: The Rational Economics of an Irrational World* (New York: Random House, 2008), and the idea about 'the hidden side of everything' from Levitt and Dubner, *Freakonomics: A Rogue Economist Explores the Hidden Side of Everything* (New York: William Morrow, 2005).

The emphasis on scarcity as defining the subject matter of economics was famously advocated by Robbins, *The Nature and Significance of Economic Science* (London: Macmillan, 1932/1984).

Friedman, 'The Methodology of Positive Economics', in *Essays in Positive Economics*, ed. M. Friedman (Chicago: University of Chicago Press, 1953) took a very strong position that the truth of assumptions is irrelevant to the assessment of a model – although his reasons were not the same as mine. McCloskey, *If You're So Smart: The Narrative of Economic Expertise* (Chicago: University of Chicago Press, 1990) is the key inspiration of my line of thinking about economics-as-metaphor.

The argument about used cars is a very famous one in economics and comes from Akerlof, 'The Market for Lemons: Quality Uncertainty and the Market Mechanism', *Quarterly Journal of Economics* 84 (1975): 488–500.

In *Capitalism and Freedom* (Chicago: University of Chicago Press, 1962), Milton Friedman achieved one of his claims to fame by opposing professional licensure along the lines suggested in chapter 3, as well as advancing many other clever arguments about the workings of the free market which have influenced what I have presented here in various ways.

The development of the efficient markets hypothesis is particularly associated with Fama, 'Efficient Capital Markets: A Review of Theory and Empirical Work', *Journal of Finance* 25.2 (1970): 383–417, and the idea that less than perfectly rational anticipations of anticipations are in practice more important, with Keynes, *The General Theory of Employment, Interest and Money* (London: Macmillan, 1936), chapter 12.

Elster, *Sour Grapes: Studies in the Subversion of Rationality* (Cambridge: Cambridge University Press, 1983) contains many of the best ideas on the limits of the 'rationality' assumption in economic analysis, including some used in the text.

The idea of 'conspicuous consumption' originates with Veblen, *The Theory of the Leisure Class* (New York: New York & Co, 1899), but was taken to a higher level by Hirsch, *The Social Limits to Economic Growth* (London: Routledge, 1977).

Many of the ideas relating 'monopoly' to innovation are derived from Schumpeter, *Capitalism, Socialism and Democracy* (London: George Allen and Unwin, 1943).

The interpretation of the problem of achieving sufficient industrial investment in the context of uncertain labour relations is derived from Lancaster, 'The Dynamic Inefficiency of Capitalism', *Journal of Political Economy* 81.5 (1973): 1092–1109.

The idea of 'efficiency wages' has various sources, but the one I had most closely in mind was Schapiro and Stiglitz, 'Equilibrium Unemployment as a Worker Disciplining Device', *American Economic Review* 74 (1984): 433–44.

The argument about educational 'signalling' comes from Spence, 'Job market signaling', *Quarterly Journal of Economics* 87.3 (1973): 355–74.

For most economists, clear thinking about the consequences of diminishing marginal product of capital, and the sharp capital/technology distinction arises in Solow, 'A Contribution to the Theory of Economic Growth', *Quarterly Journal of Economics* 70.1 (1956): 65–94, and the 'hammer' story comes from Young,

'Increasing Returns and Economic Progress', *Economic Journal* 38 (1928): 527–42.

Shin, 'Reflections on Northern Rock', *Journal of Economic Perspectives* 23.1 (2009): 101–19 analysed the failure of Northern Rock in terms of a creditor run.

Index